Wondering and Wandering of Hearts

Poems from Uganda

Edited by: Susan N. Kiguli
     Hilda J. Twongyeirwe

With a Preface by Mwalimu Austin Bukenya

A Publication of FEMRITE
Uganda Women Writers Association

FEMRITE - Uganda Women Writers Association
P.O. Box 705, Kampala
Tel: +256 414 543943 / +256 772 743943
Email: info@femriteug.org
www.femriteug.org

Wondering and Wandering of Hearts

ISBN:978-9970-480-12-8

Cover and text design Ronald Ssali
E-mail: ronalds410@gmail.com

Table of Contents

Celebrating 20 Years of Creative Engagement (1996-2016)

This volume of poetry is in honour of the valiant women and men of Uganda who have walked with FEMRITE since 1996. It has been a journey of new beginnings and exploration, a journey of immense achievement as well as challenges.

The collection celebrates not only the poets in it but the collective Ugandan soul as reflected through the pages – from the prized poets who need no introduction to younger poets with unrivalled talent and to a new generation of aspiring writers who FEMRITE has nurtured through Creative Writing Clubs in secondary schools. We acknowledge the generosity of all the contributors. FEMRITE takes responsibility for the order of poets' names in this book. This was done for purposes of uniformity.

FEMRITE steps into a new decade with renewed energy to amplify African women's literary voices and to contribute to building a vibrant literature sector in this part of the universe. Whereas fiction might not fix the broken dreams of our nations, nor cause change overnight, it stirs the conscience into reflection, rethinking, resisting and becomes a point of reference for now and for future generations.

We are most grateful to the partners who afforded the organisation a venerable celebration of the twenty years, part of which was the publishing of this collection; CKU - Denmark and Christoph Lodemann, Miles Morland, African Women's Development Fund, American Embassy, Makerere University School of Women and Gender studies under the leadership of Assoc. Prof Josephine Ahikire, Makerere University Department of Literature and Ethiopian Airlines.

To our most valued readers, allow the poetry to transport you into wondering and wandering hearts and enjoy what lies within.

Hilda J. Twongyeirwe
January 2017

Preface

I am celebrating as I write this preface. But that is not surprising. It seems it is what I have been doing as long as I have lived with FEMRITE, and that is as long as she has been around. I rejoiced when she took off in 1996. I cheered when she put out her first books and I have kept applauding as she leapt from one imaginative enterprise and adventure to another.

One might say that that was to be expected, since I have been and I am proudly and intimately part of the FEMRITE venture all along. If love begins at home, then I admit that loving FEMRITE is also loving myself. I know, too, that my love for FEMRITE is simply a reciprocation. I have always felt genuinely loved and appreciated by my sisters.

Apart from celebrating FEMRITE, however, introducing this verse collection gives me several other reasons for rejoicing. The first is that this anthology further underlines what I said when we were celebrating our twentieth anniversary. Our far-sighted founders, "Mother Hen" Mary Karooro and her colleagues, got it right when they set out to encourage us to write. There were in 1996, and there still are today, many voices demanding and deserving to be heard. Through such publications as this anthology, FEMRITE is enabling us to hear these voices, and she will go on enabling us to hear these and many other deserving voice.

Secondly, I am overwhelmed by the sheer range of topics, themes and sentiments covered by the poems in this anthology. There is a general misconception among large sections of people that poetry is an expression of only a few privileged experiences, most notoriously romantic love. An anthology like this one goes a long way to disprove this. Poetry is, as we should know, about life, the whole range of life.

The authors featured here live up to the billing by covering a stunning variety of human experience, aspiration and reflection. Love does feature, as it should, but what we have mostly here is not the cheap sentimentality of the two-cent pop rap.

Rather, the poets explore the niches and nuances of relationships from a startling variety of angles: desire, search, pain, joy, loss and salvation. Indeed, what you might at first sight take for a straight "love poem" ends up opening into a whole new world of historical, political or spiritual contemplation. Social issues are often tackled head-on, the poets searing and scorching in their satire and sarcasm or in the bluntness of their criticism.

Most of the pieces dissect with profound incisiveness and eloquent lucidity the challenging times in which most of them have grown up, prominent among these being the Northern Uganda insurgency, which has impacted on all of us more profoundly than commonly acknowledged. Indeed, going by the gist of the verses recorded here, this is one of the defining experiences of the generation of the first quarter of the twenty-first century.

But often the voices rise high above experience and history-specific concerns to cosmic philosophical contemplation. "Your existence," writes one of the young poets, "is one big negotiation/between the years and your body." I had never thought of life like that, but it is a plausible way of defining our existential struggle. It reminds one of Alexander Pope's view of poetry as "what oft was thought, but never so well-expressed."

Another especially satisfying feature of this anthology is the generous representation of male poets. This vindicates the claim of our FEMRITE sisters, right from its foundation, that they had nothing against their literary brothers. Their primary purpose was simply the rectification of the balance in the publishing world, where the woman's voice was rarely and only grudgingly heard. Now that the sisters are actually the dominant voice on Uganda's literary scene, they have no qualms about sharing the platform with their like-minded brothers.

But, as I know to my profit and joy, exclusiveness has never been a part of FEMRITE's way of doing things. Otherwise, how would I have come to be a founding (honorary) member of this distinguished sorority? Moreover, from its earliest days, FEMRITE has devised and implemented outreach programmes that have included both female and male writers. Among these have been the Writers' Caravan and the exceptionally successful Monday evening weekly readings, at which most of the pieces in this anthology were first presented and workshopped.

But the happiest aspect of this anthology for me is the dexterity and polish of the compositions of many of the young poets included. As I have said elsewhere, this refinement is, obviously, not accidental. It is the result of dedicated and systematic hard work, which is a sine-qua-non of all good writing. The young people's seriousness in this direction is a heart-warming vindication of my lifelong advocacy of technique in creativity.

I am endlessly on record as insisting that strong feelings, ardent social concern or a burning desire to communicate, and the like, are important, but they are not enough to produce artistic writing, especially verse. To turn all these into a viable text, the writer has to display competent language use, meticulous patterning and organization and a "startling" imagination that turns concepts into leaping, palpable pictures.

Of course, all writing, and especially verse writing is experimental. No experiment can be said to be perfect, because it is, by definition, a process. Moreover, it would be unrealistic to expect a uniform level of excellence across such a wide variety of experiments as represented in this anthology. But, going by the best of the daring verse assays (and essays) presented here, I can confidently predict that the future of Ugandan poetry is bright.

Mwalimu Austin Bukenya
FEMRITE Honorary Member
Simba Cottage, Gayaza-Kyetume
10 February 2017

W-W-Woman

(For FEMRITE@20)
Mwalimu Austin Bukenya

Whence, weary woman, wailing, worn with work
Immersed in muted misery and mired in murk
In worry, wormy weals of whips and weeds
Of custom, crooked culture, creaky creeds,
Denied a voice, a visage, even a name,
Will fair fortune flare upon your frail frame?

Why, weeping waif, await wizard winds
To chase away the haunting taunting fiends
That bind, and bend and bound and blight
Your life, your love, your right, your light?

When, wounded womb, will wisdom, will
And steely nerve ascend the craggy hill
Assert your power, pain and pointed pact
To be, to do, to grow, be free, impact?

This poem was presented on 28th July 2016 at the School
of Women and Gender Studies at the Opening Ceremony of
the FEMRITE Literature Conference to celebrate 20 years of
dedicated service to the literary arts.

Don't ask me again

Prossy Abalo

It is not for you,
My father answered me,
When I inquired about school.

Instead he taught me
To welcome my brothers with peace
As they returned from school
To listen with sanity
As they narrated stories of school.

When I protested
My own father called me shit
He compared me to a bitch
He said I was a mere girl
Education was a waste of time
Not a requirement for roles of girls.

Then one day my aunt visited
She preached the gospel of free education
The gospel of education for all
The blind, the deaf, the lame and mentally ill
She became the oil in my father's ears
He finally sent me to school.

I struggled when my name was read
I could not comprehend concepts
My age became a laughter line for classmates
I was their kick ball on the playground.

Today their eyes widen in wonder
Seeing me standing in front of the dock
Checking files with ease
Asking and directing tough questions
Verdict after verdict
A mere girl
Acquitting the innocent
sentencing the guilty.

Doleful Sunsets

Richard Aboko

Darkness is sitting down.
The heart beats faster as the sun goes to sleep.
It's time to spread dirty rags, torn-up sacks,
Lie down.
If lucky, cover the body from smiling mosquitoes.

Big explosions.
Everyone looks at each other.
I look up in the sky,
Desolation.

The listening night is filled with sounds of coughing-
I join the choir.

The sky cracks its bones.
The wind hums offensively.
The heavy clouds break loose;
a fearful storm erupts.
The lull after the storm alerts the ears for whistling
bullets.
Our feet get to rapid dialogue,
Only to rest in the trap.

Sunshine smile

Acaye Pamela Elizabeth

You keep visiting the graveyard!
What are you looking for in yesterday's litter?

Renew your spirit and set forth with the dawn.
Blow the *Agwara* horn again through your split lips.
Stop visiting the graveyard to disturb spirits long dead
As you mourn over a yester sun that will never return.
Listen to the wind whispering your name!

Nobody wants to know your pain.
The smooth skin on your deep scars just intrigues them.
Nobody wants to know your pain;
Just tell them why your eyes dance in their sockets
like *Nkejje* fish swirling in a pond,
With your laughter arresting the room like a thunderbolt!
They want to know why you smile with a glitter of
tears in your eyes and,
A softening of the ever moist tender flesh that
borders your lips:

Nobody wants to know your pain!
Just tell them the story of your smile;
Tell it with a cup of lemon grass and ginger tea to share.
Today is here and it must be lived with the living.

Letter to the Morning

Acaye Pamela Elizabeth

Dear morning, thank you for caressing my eyes open
with your dawn.
My night was as long as the 14 months of
spontaneous silence from him,
Whose ghost returned to haunt me yesterday night!
You see, when the evening dressed itself in black,
The shadow of our convulsive relation attacked the
door of my mind.

"Breathe, breathe baby mama!" I counseled myself.
Open up your pancreas and breathe!
But this night must die!
I clenched my fists and buried the darkness into the grave!
The sun showed up this morning,
It pried my clenched fists open;
Here I am, brewing myself a cup of African tea:
Half milk to replenish my lost joy and half water to
cleanse my being of sorrow.
I am adding a pinch of fresh ginger to refresh my
mind and,
A bay leaf to inspire healing;
Two teaspoons of sugar, I will add to smile my day,
And with a satisfied sip of my tea, I will drink to a
brand new day!
Good morning.

Peace

Vicky Achiro

The village has risen
We are all looking for you
Are you lost in the bushy neighbourhood?
You used to be here then you went missing
When are you returning?
When will you be back to give us freedom
We have been told that there's peace
But you don't hear peace
Peace is seen
All we see is round-bellied men behind office desks
Peace is felt
All our wounded hearts feel is restlessness
With our Children strapped on our backs
Play in this land has became a luxury
Please ask for directions and return.

Voice of my people

Gloria Adoch

The voice of my people is as loud as the ngalabi drum,
Yet it's not heard beyond the edge of village
A big wall seems to stand between us and our leaders,
We are a forgotten village
A dying soul.

We too want peace,
But portions seem so limited they can't go round.
Some people have become greedy with what belongs to all?

The voice of my people is lonely like that of a
mistreated child.
Might we be step children?
Our voice has not been heard
Yet it is as loud as a roaring lion *Wii-Anaka*
As rough as the jack fruit and *kitafeli* skin in our
compounds.

The Toilet
Earnest Ainembabazi

Keep it clean and you will not regret entering,
Make it dirty, and regret your entry.

When you are out, you crave to enter
Those who are inside crave to get out.

If marriage is different,
Then I did not write this

The Fair God

Earnest Ainembabazi

God was fair to create us in his image.
But how many images has he?
HE must have various sizes
Heights and
Colour.
Since HE is everything
We can be anything.

Age of consent

Melvin Vincent Akankwasa

I woke up this morning
And yes I did feel different
At the back of my mind
A number is ringing
Oh I am eighteen!

I can now drive
I can now consent to marriage
I can sit at men's table
I can thrust my fist in the air and speak
I can...

I jump out of bed and reach for mum's car keys
But she won't trust me with her car
I sit at table with men
Their talk turns me into stone

I set out to find my bride
But realise I have nowhere to house her
It's then it dawns on me
Age is just a number.

If I had the moon in my hands...

Charlotte Akello

I would climb the sky
and visit the stars
Tell them a story
That will make them smile.

I would visit the world in a few hours,
Read everyone's story
Without judging them,
Hold their hands and read their mind.

I wouldn't let them run away
Like they always do
I would grab them
And give them the company they long for.

I wouldn't focus on myself this time,
I would see the despair in their faraway eyes
And wipe away the uncried tears
Pick up pieces of broken hearts.

If I had the moon in my hands,
I would walk and light your dark world
Keep the moon so bright
That you have no reason to be sad.

I would smile with love,
And take all nitty gritty pieces of your life,

I would make them into a story
That's worth sharing.

If I had the moon in my hands,
I would fly over and walk with you
You would feel my presence and support
If I had the moon in my hands,
I would tear up the sky to see that smile again.

If I had the moon in my hands,
I would do all I can
For I would own this world.

Poet's Mind

Charlotte Akello

The trees sway
Getting your attention
Your mind wonders at
The beauty of creation
The beauty of nature.

The new moon comes
It triggers an emotion in you
Wants to say something
Wants you to speak
Leaves you wondering.

Your brother's blood cries in South Africa
As it clots in the cold soil
Heavy from unshed tears
You decide to keep a memory
Let me think today...
Maybe write tomorrow.

The tomorrow you waited for is today
Your sister's and brother's souls burn for unknown
reasons.
Souls of Garrisa students cry out
You still await the best words.

Then comes Nigeria and Sudan
Brothers holding grudges against one another

Slaughtering each other like animals
Staining the soil with curses.

Your neighbour dies in child-birth
A child is raped and no justice given
A new moon comes in a different way each month
Bearing a new story

Your pen is rusty
Your paper is dusty
Your mind is clogged
It too carries unshed tears
The correct words still do not come

You just grab your pen and paper
You just say it
You get done with it
You are a voice.

Land of Hope

Brenda Rachel Alaroker

My tribe,
Acholi,
Is a people of dignity
A land of beauty
Though it suffered the 20-year LRA war
It remains a land of hope
It's a niche of the best of all.
Acholi,
My pride,
Our dark skin is our identity
The depth of who we are
My priority.

The Acholi's Vexation

Ivan Aloya

Fire tongues from
Late evening shootings
Rolls of smoke rising from the huts
Early morning tears, tear down the faces of inhabitants

Unbearable cries from women pierce the sky
They sob
For children captured in the last raid

The captives suffer
Walking barefooted
Neck-breaking loads on their heads
Hunger and misery, their companions
Weak slaughtered like goats for the evening meal

The government seems in deep slumber
Eyes closed to the North
Its back to the North
Its face to the capital city
Snoring away questions
Was Northern even part of Uganda?
Will the blast cease to bite?

Our Father

Harriet Anena

Dear mother,

You call me a slut for conceiving at 14

Insult me for bringing shame upon your home

For growing up unpruned like a tree among weeds

"What kind of child knows a man before her breasts sprout?"

"What kind of child loves a man more than food?"

Ask me mother, interrogate me for my immorality

Call me a teenage whore

Banish me

Curse my child and wish me a miscarriage

My child and I, share the same father

I Am A Poem

Harriet Anena

Make me your music
Sing me
Roll me on your tongue like unforgettable lyrics
Make me your dance moves
Take me to tiny little heavens with the left, right,
back, forth of your steps
Breathe me in, slowly.
Open your eyes, slowly. Then look at the world. It
belongs to us.
Now, detonate me. Break me into tiny little pieces
that only you can glue back.
Because I am your song. So sing me.
I am a poem. Recite me.

Tame My Tears

Harriet Anena

If I must cry for your lowly peasants Lord,
Tame my tears and save my mascara from ruin
If I must cry for the 16 mothers who die daily in child birth
Pat my back and rescue my face from wrinkles
If I must weep for the shoeless pupils in Mpigi
Keep my head up so the camera doesn't miss my
        national grief
If I must cry for donor aid that grew legs and fled our
        Treasury
Hold my hand, Lord
And defend my country from global shame

I am an African

Bruce Arinaitwe

I am African,
An African who belongs to the land
Of the black
Of the strong
Of the wise
I have a right to the rites of the land
I hold conversations with trees
I speak to the soil and hills and valleys
I speak to the waters and the winds
Skies share secrets with me
Cows and hens too, share their knowledge
Picked from songs and riddles
Picked from norms and rituals that grace African
compounds

My Tongue

Bruce Arinaitwe

With my tongue I tore off your clothes,
I spread you naked in public.
I did not know that time would come...
I am sorry.

With my tongue I took your friends away.
With words more poisonous than venom,
I spoke dirt about your name.
I was a fool.

I spoke about you to the public,
I told them things.
How your mother balanced baskets of Irish potatoes
          on her head
Looking for nothing but a one thousand shillings note.

I spoke of your father too.
How he used to beat up your mother.
How he dressed in one pair of trousers like a cockroach
How his t-shirt dried on his shoulders.

I told stories of how you used to time meal times at our home,
How you ate leftovers
How I pulled your hair, abused you, slapped you.
But you still came each lunch time uninvited.
I spoke
I did not know that time would come...
And I search
For the stone that builders had cast away.

Wed my heart

Bonnetvanture Asiimwe

I gathered myself and sat searching
what can stifle my heart
And perhaps
Find favour in my sight.

I remembered Nikki Giovanni
courting poetry:
…poets are beyond love.
And I said:
Sad news indeed!

I will wed my heart.
And turn into art.

Conception

Bonnetvanture Asiimwe

Two sculptors springing
from the darkness of conception
Sat like me here
And hollowed their hearts to harness beauty
And crown wonders of a woman in two sculptures.

One made her a grotesque figurine,
A trader who knows her trade
And treasures her merchandise
That she displays her possessions precariously
Like displayed paper sheets
Just like bait that hides a hook…

On the other relief,
Two African women
Sculpted on a shield like slate
Look out at whoever cares to see them,
With heads bald, hair hovering like saints' crown
Made of metallic slabs,
Eyes keen and questioning
Why they must be made billboards
To advertise their status:
Married, Widowed, Engaged, Raped,
Destroyed, Done with, Damaged…

As I am wondering why schooled dons
Allowed the two sculptors install

The works in the heart of the school's compound,
I remember what one taught me:
Things are never seen as beautiful or ugly,
But are rather judged by the omniscient viewer
According to the way they demarcate themselves
against space...
We always want to see things fit in spaces we allocate them
Unfortunately time always change their shape and form!

Apathy

Jackie Asiimwe

Apathy
That rolling of the eyes
That pssssh
Whatever
That leave me alone
Pulizzz!

Apathy
Total lack of telepathy
Failing to see the signs of the times
Because we do not know
That times have signs

Apathy
That kill me slowly
With sweet nothings
You want another rap?
The growing accustomed
To the status quo
Going with the flow
Flowing as we go

Apathy
That disease
That will bring us
To our knees
That do as you please
'Kasita twebaka ku tulo'

Apathy
That which we must shake off
Wake up!
Smell the coffee people!
Uganda is on fire!
Get busy before you burn
Before you have only ashes
To turn over
To the next generation

(03/07/13)

Kasita twebaka ku tulo means at least we have some sleep

Why must I pay tax?

Jackie Asiimwe

Why must I pay tax? I ask
When all I see is –
Garbage overflowing
Potholes growing
Teachers yawning
Kids not learning
Doctors frowning
Nurses striking
Districts multiplying
Services dying
State House budget rising
While the shilling is falling

Why must I pay tax? I ask
When what I pay is stolen
Court cases are stalling
The thieves keep rolling
As they go on boasting
About 'Falling into things'
Why must I pay tax? I ask

(09/26/2015)

Heartbreak

Regina Asinde

You broke my heart again---
you took the chef's salad knife
and carved it into intricate pieces
that seem to fit but never really fit---
last time you diced it up
and blended it in the mixer;
I swore it would never bleed again
I was wrong---
the glue that holds the pieces seeps through…
answer me, I beg;
was the pleasure you derived
as intense as the pain
that sizzles through my nerves
like chilli thrown into boiling oil?

I seek to remember

Regina Asinde

the mist that drapes
the sightless sky
embraces my mind hard
like an opened freezer
 hissing fiercely
swirling in my mind
blurring my vision.

when I strain eyes hard
squinting to catch faraway pictures,
I see but shady patches:
Pictures that flicker
trying to push through the memories
of a life before the booming air
like a radio station tuned off frequency.

I see but
crimson shades of burning thatches,
Striking machete strokes
as life flows out mutilated bodies.
the grey tones of the mist reveal no sky-blue.
only gloomy firmaments of charred villages
stand before the mist conceals.

I seek to remember
life before the booming air.

I am a fragmented body:
underneath the new flesh
debris of shattered bones still pierce.

I am a body
that has forgotten how to heal self

Hard as many try to help me mend
but the mist rattles so hard
and though I seek to remember
I cower in their shadows.

I seek to remember
life before the booming air.

I will undress now

Regina Asinde

Piece by piece
I will remove them
I will undo them now.
I will undress now like the stripper
you wish me to be
I will throw them at you
Daring you to grab them
Measuring how vast your desire is
Seeing your indecision on whether
To hold the pieces
Or touch my nakedness.

 I will gently remove my starched headpiece
That sits like a queen on my head
and finger comb my shaggy shrubby hair
knotted on my head.
I will undress now
For why should I hide my beauty
from your loving eyes?

I will, with particular care, unclasp my gold earrings
That have winked all night at you
and leave dark scarred earlobes
I will undress now
For why should I hide
My beauty from your yearning eyes?

I will unadorn my neck
Tugging away the heavy priceless pearls
that have hung around my neck
and leave my almost invisible neck bare
I will undress now
For why should I hide my beauty
from your revering eyes?

I will, with precision and concision, unclasp
my floral printed blouse that has
fitted me to perfection all evening
To reveal my wrinkled saggy breasts
That have obeyed the law of gravity
For why should I hide my beauty
from your thirsting eyes?

I will slowly push my pencil skirt
That has hugged my curves like kid gloves
I will sway with it as it travels down
Revealing flabby cellulite infected folds of flesh
For why should I hide my beauty
from your deifying eyes?

I will undress now
Piece by piece
For my beauty
Is what really glazes your eyes
Isn't it?

To be child again

Lillian Akampurira Aujo

Your dreams are dark lakes
sanctuaries of reminiscence

here
you don't have to prove
                        you know
            you're beautiful,
here
you simply are
floating in old knowing
swimming without trying
paddling in abundant answers
here
where it's irrelevant to remember questions
                        why ask them
when they were anticipated for you?
like   your breath would need air
these answers were always here
you simply had to return
to child again.

A meaning to birth

Lillian Akampurira Aujo

1

I
before awareness
floated in a certain vestigial existence
chromosomes threading
cells dividing
thriving in your fecund womb
sponging life from you

you said my first step
was a mark in your world
I wish I could understand
the myriad shades of that imprint

you felt my first grip
a feeble instinct
to hold on to a life
that at times seems illusive

you know how my first word
 shaped the silence
so who am I
to shatter it?

2

Every man shapes the air around him
curves a space
for his form

but every woman
while tracing the air around her
curves two spaces
one for her form
and another for her child's form
again, and again, and again ...

3

The man sows a seed in the garden
the seed grows into a plant
that blossoms into flowers
the man picks the flowers
and uproots the plant
the soil remembers
the pattern of the roots
that once grew in it
the roots miss the soil
they once grew in
and the man,
who remembers the man?

4

Perhaps when a piece of you
dropped off and fell
I began to grow

like spear grass in the Savannah
verdantly spreading
in an endless search
for likenesses with my father

5
I wake up to beauty,
to eyes deeper than clear wells,
to laughter purer than the deepest springs,
to a chromatic gaze of the man who left:
loving you could be so hard
yet loving you is simple still

Of suicidal mad men and gates of heaven

Lillian Akampurira Aujo

Suppose one day you saw the world through God's
eyes and spied
the mad man of Kasubi at his corner by the undone
storied building,
the building whose wooden planks and timber surge
with the weight of dried cement
calcifying riches. Suppose you heard the end of the
world in his voice as he howled
and howled, at the opulence that's been dangled at
him and at the gnawing hunger
his most trusted companion

Suppose the next day he was still there a still photograph
'un-fadable' by wind, sun or rain bony knees cutting
the air around him like knives a wound as wide as a lake
where his ankle used to be. but this time
this time he was singing about swatting flies
from juicy wounds and waiting
and waiting for his last breath

Would you show him to the last story
and point him to the loosest scaffolding?
would you ask him if that's why he always sat there?
would you meet the glazed over concrete in his eyes
as you told him
that the gates of heaven don't really open for suicidal
mad men?

Catharsis

Lillian Akampurira Aujo

When you died
I feared to close my eyes
because I was scared
that your face would slip
into that space of nothingness.

I groped through our memories
fed them to our dwindling fire:
it was the best kindling I could find
to keep the darkness out

so now I sleep with the ghost of you
and the ghost of our love:
at least they keep a shadow
of a smile on my face.

World Armageddon

Lillian Akampurira Aujo

1

Sometimes we think
it's one long nightmare
Uzis and AKs
firing in sporadic glory
taking turns to cheer
exploding bombs and missiles

we think it a bad joke
the thousand pixels of blood
splitting into millions
before they come together
(on the screen)
for us to see the news –
another beheading
by a headless phantom:

and there's what they want you to think
so that you don't hurry to awake
from the mythos of ideology
so open your eyes already,
this is the stuff of your reality.

2

We heard the girls were taken from their homes
and the law married them to men of God
men whose virtuousness was so deserving
of gifts like virgins of nine years or so

we shouted the message to birds in treetops
to slogan our anger and heartbreak
'Bring back our girls! Bring back our girls'

we saw them blaze schools and churches
slaughter men, rape women – like those deeds
would grant them passage to redemption
when the land was cleansed

we scoffed at their ideology:
this was a war in the heads of foolish people
how do you win a war with a foolish man?

so we sat at a Union and discussed
how to stay in power;
the terrorist Armageddon could wait.

3
After 70 years
Auschwitz sits
a heavy stone
on the conscience of history

Hitler – Amin – Kony –
what else
is waiting
to happen?
And how shall we live
with a history
that's buried her conscience?

Strikethrough

Sophie Bamwoyeraki

Sweating. Faltering steps.
Visitor 0069 approached the desk.
The cow bulging in his jacket pocket
This umpteenth envelope landed on the desk.
Officer TMK in a well-timed swoop of a kite spirited
it off;
The khaki affair slid into the drawer
Huddling in the corner with the other cows.

Officer TMK stole a glance at his colleagues.
Like a schoolboy learning to cross a street
Looked Left. Right. Then Left again. The way was
clear.
He took a peek. Re-arranged the cows in order.
With a chief tester's smile, he nodded in satisfaction.

The short list was a ladder to the sky.
Names. Names. Names...
Bachelors. Diplomas. Certificates...
All well-qualified. All well-read. All sharp...
He picked up a black pen.

~~Linda Mukama.~~ Pecunia Nsimbi.

'You're unqualified,' lying convincingly,
For the eavesdroppers' interest. 'Try again next year.'

Visitor 0069 marched out.

His visitor's tag swinging. Left. Right. Left.

His laughing footfalls could be heard in the corridor.

With his heart soaring like an eagle

Officer TMK texted the jewellery shop, car, and land dealers

To conclude pending business…

The CCTV camera installed over the weekend

Captured every action, every movement, every unspoken word.

Relief

Sophie Bamwoyeraki

Planted a seed just like others
Watered it just like others
Waited patiently just like others
One year, two years, fifteen.

New cycle signs. Impromptu visitors
Longed for by others, were sharp steel daggers.
New cycle signs, stalking me day and night
Accused me of crimes uncommitted,
Labelled me with names uncalled for.

My flat waist became my face
Questions from my in-laws shocked and irked me.
My husband's violent anger turned me into a
punching bag
I longed to flee to furrow. To flee.

A dreary sky hung over me
No sun seeped through
No raindrop spared a thought.
I invented stories to explain the scars
My salty emotions went unheard

Then one day he turned into a cargo ship.
New address. New life.

A tale of despair. A dappled mind.
No pulsation.
Uprooted. No water. No sunshine.

Time is a mystery.
Time is abrasive.
Repairing broken hearts.
As I look back now, vibrant, solo
The helm of my heart
Glistens and glitters like a gilded trophy.

The Inescapable

Violet Barungi

I don't mind growing old
It is the natural order of things
But I strongly object
To all aches and pains
Taking refuge
In every nook and crack
Of my beleaguered body

I highly resent the fact
That my once torch-like eyes
Surreptitiously grow dim
Denying me the pleasure
I get from reading books

O yes I abhor
My uncoordinated motions
That belie the claims
That I once was
The wizard of the spoon-egg race

I demand accountability
Of all the money spent
On various stay-young products
By Avon, Clinique
Jergens and L'oreal
Collagen creams
Anti-ageing moisturisers

All religiously applied
Have all come to naught
With nothing to show for the effort
But an empty purse
And accelerated damage to sheathe

No, let me make it clear
I have no objection
To growing old
But I strongly resent
Being encumbered
With defective equipment
Whose purpose
Is only historical

TRAITOR

Bwambale Steven Mugati

It was well when we started.

Our blood flowed
Ceaselessly in each other's veins
We all meant well.
But lo! A blindfold!
A promise of wealth turned you against us.
With our foes you dined and laughed
Our throes your bliss.
Wealth filled your lips
One by one we diminished.
Indiscriminately earth partook of us
Your   compound was filled with scents of rich oils.
You changed cars like clothes.
When you walked your feet did not touch the ground.
You became blind about the stained reputation you built.

And us,

We prayed for vengeance.
We sought justice.
We prayed and fasted.
And before long
You had turned pauper.
All your worldly treasures were no more.
You turned to us for solace
But it was too late.
Your devil companion forsook you too.

You died miserably
And we hope to hell you went
Where you always belonged.

The Lady I Knew

Richard Chole

I lower myself quite hesitantly
to sit across the table
to face her steady gaze
of languid weary blood-shot eyes – telltale of fast life
and long nights gone by.
Porcelain shine of slick nails – well packaged
urban sophistication for contractual relationship
calculatedly closing to clasp glass of Coke,
perhaps, bore~d I couldn't fill it with red wine.
She flinches at my eager query
to discern how far she's come
and chose intuition for my Nokia brand
with practiced eyes to place a price tag on me –
her scanned highest bidder.

I recall her fervent erstwhile way of life full,
vitality pulsed sunny smile of her eyes,
radiance to verve and charm the universe
her scream when she finally hit eighteen,
delight of a lifetime's dream –
to embrace the world
and take it away with her
but the wild seized and swept her headlong,
off the sheltered haven of instruction
sworn to mould her take on the world.
There, did her credulous wit carry her
to the promise of bliss, enchantment

on the paved lanes and lights of the city –
nirvana of throbbing heartbeats
and there found her fulfillment
of Womanhood and Wisdom.

Her glossy coated lips draw backwards
peeling over shiny teeth in stale routinely rehearsed smile.
But nature has its ways round our simulation:
furrows on her face deepen – youth gone hastily old,
each tired groove a tale of failure,
betrayal, deflowerment, bitterness,
shame, tragedy, love gone sore, vengeance,
pain masked with hard-boiled cynicism and scorn,
a beautified menace to life.

Jungle

Richard Chole

Towering trees, like Ra's temple pillars on the Nile,
Gnarling branches, holding canopies like Hercules.

Leaping apes, like a jungle pantomime.
Snarling leopard, with flashing canines
And eyes of fire!

Hapless rabbit,
Entwined in the mighty sinewy
Of the African Bore.

Terrifying beauty of the green serpent,
Slithering through foliage
In search of prey

Icy water fall,
Cascading white sheet
Over grey boulders
To flash fine spray
And bare miniature rainbow
In the evening sunray.

Darkness falls,
Distant cries of retreating birds,
Drip! drip! drip! of water,
Croaking of the frog
And hooting of the lone owl
In the eerie silence
Of the night of the jungle.

Not Real

Janny Ekyasiimire

Death is not real
If It were real
Heaven would be a myth
And Jesus would not have risen

Death is not real
If it were real
It would not be part of life
And life is alive.

Death is not real
If it were real
Then we would have no soul
But is it real that death is unreal?

I wait upon thee

David Patrick Emiru

Here where we were two rivers flowing differing courses,
Where we were two sonnets separated by a page
And I, was about your curves and bends
And you, about life by the banks, and the smell of roses.

Here where droplets of my lapping progress fell on the
    bed of your unscripted courteousness,
Where my peeping hyphens,
 Lent Expression to your syllables thro' the fold-lines of age,
Where we were about anything: curves and bends, life by the banks,
    the smell of roses, homelessness…!

I wait upon thee
Here where the sound of our blissful drum on rocks
    turned seas into whisperers of stories,
And suns into ethereal cities
Here were our souls leaped thro' the pages of the ages;
    sonnets, limericks, epitaphs, thro' humanity!

A note on the padlock (the bits of love)

David Patrick Emiru

On entry, you'll find the gallows erected on the sands
        of homelessness,
The garments like loose nooses_
Hanging over torn draperies,
And the black seams of silence sealing-in the
        could-have-beens within this shelter.

The will must've kept bits of love in the granaries

Or under the pilling dust. The fading prints lead a trail
Into the only room, in a corner, you'll see the twiggy
        embers of a dead_
Fire, the ashes cast like sheets of white fibre,
And besides the hearth-stones, smithereens shaped
        into a heart.

The will must've spent bits of love feeding the fire

Or building a face to these walls. On them, you'll see
        sooted memories
Climbing the branches of shady reveries,
The petals paled & fallen
Looking into heaven's eyes and tender derris crawling
        into pots filled in nothingness.

The will must've left bits of love to the bidding of the heavens

And nothing to the heart of this dwelling; but you'll
        hear echoes of a broken thumb-piano,

The visiting mirages of the should-have-beens by the
        bedside floor,
And the seams of cemetery_
Silence slithering thro' the chords of a should-be song.

Wo-man

Laban Erapu

You may not know me from Adam
But I am your -man
Born of your need to be complete
Spawned in your solitude
Flesh of your flesh, blood of your blood!

I may not look good enough
To eat for a weekend dinner
I may not be rich enough
To buy you the world to play with
I may not be eloquent enough
To charm your heart away
But I am your -man
Like no other can ever be
I am flesh of your flesh
I am blood of your blood.

Wo- sounds like a woeful cry without the -man
To make a complete wo-man of you
For your name was bonded with mine
Since Adam and Eve
Meant to be mine since Creation
Wo- I am your -man
And Wo-man you are us together forever!

When I call you Woman
Know that it's not out of disrespect

But because I'm proud of what you are to me
Knowing as I do that without you
Wo-man, there's no us or me!

Queen of Queens

Laban Erapu

I have seen a thousand seasons
and more
I have blossomed and withered
I have been born and reborn
I have lived many lives
Iremera
Nyabiingi
Nyakaima
Nyinamwiiru
and many many more
East or West - where haven't I been?
North or South - what is there that I haven't seen?

I have seen kingdoms come and kingdoms go
I have known kings and I have been consort to kings
my loins have borne princes and princesses of the royal house.

I have bequeathed many a legacy
always protected my own jealously
and laid a heavy hand on those
who earned my wrath:
power, wealth, fame
I have had them all
Love, fear, anger
I know them all
I am every woman
who ever lived

or loved and lost
Nothing under the sun
or out of darkness
bothers me anymore!

She's the Sunshine of My Life

Laban Erapu

She's the sunshine of my life
This maiden that comes from the East
With the soft light of dawn
And the tenderness of youth
That swept me off my feet.

Each morning as I bathe
In the radiant rays of her smile
It's this that warms me to the new day
And I thank my lucky stars
For this gift that comes from the East.

At noon with the sun overhead
I sit in the shade of her protective care
Dreaming of the happy hours gone by
And the happy hours yet to come
As I relax in sweet contentment.

Dusk approaches on tiptoe
Blending with the melody of her voice
To fire my blood with the sun's crimson
A reminder of the youth gone by
And of a long life well lived!

Feelings Are Babies

Sam Zinunula Iga

Feelings are babies
Yes, feelings are babies
Sometimes coming to us by accident
Just out of a little incident
A meeting we thought of no consequence
Ballooning to occupy large space.

Feelings are babies
Yes, feelings are babies.
We often want them to come
We all want to have some
We patiently watch them grow
A tenderness, a twitch, a warm glow.

Some feelings grow into naughty boys
That break and destroy their toys
Shattering all arrangements we have laid
Seeming ungrateful for all efforts made
And often we wish it was different
But then babies are babies.

How Life Can Be Had

Sam Zinunula Iga

A swing of the limbs
A grasp of the vitals
A gasp of scents
A smacking of the lips
A savouring of flavours

A walk in the garden
An inspiration of air
A bask in the sun
A walk in the rain
A swim in the river
A soak in the waters

A harvest of grain
A nibble on the ears
A stroking of teats
A squirt of milk

A pounding of the heart
A throb in the veins
A pouring of sweats

An insertion
An ingestion
A digestion
Imbibation

Oh!
How life can be had.

Hand Me The Burdizzo

Sam Zinunula Iga

I want to take the bull by the scrotum
I want to squeeze it where it hurts
Not by the horny part
That is dead tissue.

I want to hang on and pull
People, hand me the burdizzo
I want the political bull to feel my anger and power
And even if it kicks me in the teeth
It will be left without doubt
That I can endanger its children.

If I Were to Die Today

Peter Mutanga Kagayi

To die today with toddlers
And mothers in the lifeless arms of nurses and doctors
Raped, draped in indifference
Scrapped in waste of empty promises expired in slums
Slumped in city mortuaries label them rotten sanctuaries

To die today with famished dreams
Famished hopes
Decaying sunsets
Decaying feet
Emptied in the escape of yesterday's generation
Angry at the omnipresence
Of our impotence

To die today, like yesterday
I would be glad for it

I would beg for it.

To whom it may concern

Peter Mutanga Kagayi

I once forgot a poem
On a bus.

I left it
In the conductor's eyes
Perched
In reflection

Of a passenger's tears
And sighs-

She had left
Her fare behind.

He slapped her.

I once forgot
A poem on a bus.

If you must know

Peter Mutanga Kagayi

Revolving mistakes make recurrent appearances in
          our mindsets.
A mind possesses no toes but how it runs, or tiptoes,
Unannounced, avoiding detection
Like it knows history is a virtue not a lesson,
We write memories to delete unpleasant scenes of our deeds
To delete our discomforting personalities
To delete memories to delete our nightmares
We write to delete such opposing ideologies
To delete such consciousness
To delete such mental madness
We write to delete we.

Revolving hand gestures make recurrent overtures to
          show our restlessness
Hands have no heart but can hold the gun
And extend membership to the *Kiboko* squad
In the same spirit
We flash hand-gestures to forgive our history – *Amandla*
We flash hand gestures not to miss our next meal
While protesting change while screaming 'No Change!'
We flash hand gestures protesting institutional pain
To delete such opposing ideologies
We flash hand gestures to delete such consciousness
To delete such mental madness
We flash to delete we.

Revolving sounds resonate in our air but silence is
   not one of them.
Listen –silence was arrested and safe-housed
When our playwrights were murdered;
What died was not the play but the personae of perception
But – guns have no consciousness and poems have no bullets
So we write words to conceal our fear for tomorrow
We write words to convene strength to fight our sorrows
We write words to give ourselves meaning to avoid
   writing plays
To avoid death
We write to delete such opposing ideologies
To delete such consciousness
To delete such mental madness
We write to delete we.

Revolving writings resonate badly like mango juice and
   beer
Like a well read poem,
Dead,
Hung by the noose
But that's no cause for a tear
Sometimes the best thing you can have is having
   nothing to fear
Sometimes the soul will persevere
Sometimes you will run into your luck, and a poem
   you write
Peers into your future
Sometimes a poem is just a poem
And needs not to be written

Sometimes writing is just not worth it
Sometimes it's a priceless gift

But if you must know
We write to delete such opposing ideologies
We write to delete such consciousness
To delete such mental madness

We write to delete we.

You Dare Not

Danson S. Kahyana

You dare not walk in this city
Sure you are safe on the pavement –
The *bodaboda* men will invade you
And fly-walk you to the orthopaedics.

You dare not use the zebra-crossing
Even if the law gives you the right of way –
Numerous people have perished there
And the state has not cared a bit.

You dare not use your phone in public
Imagining you live in a safe country –
Someone will slap you hard and hot
And run away with your precious gadget.

You dare not go to government hospitals
Expecting service deserving of citizens –
Medics will send you to private pharmacies
For its ages since public hospitals had medicine.

You dare not expect much from the National assembly
Hoping the welfare of the citizens is its priority –
That House is inhabited by all sorts of characters
Their eyes transfixed on their monthly cheques.

You dare not dream of a prosperous future
Sure your First Class will land you a juicy job –
There are strict orders from above
The interview panel dare not disregard.

Building a Decaying House
Danson S. Kahyana

The physical design –
Belligerence.

The contractor –
The executive.

The porters –
Shilling-drugged supporters of the regime.

The foundation –
Strategic constitutional amendments.

The walls –
Farcical elections.

The roof –
Disappearance of 'trouble-makers'.

The furnishing –
Mediocrity in every sector.

Two Global Villagers

Danson S. Kahyana

I

He woke up one morning
And felt like going to Africa
To escape the terrible winter
That was roasting his butt.

He picked his credit card
Bought an airticket on his iphone
Checked in online
And rushed to the airport.

In the next three hours
He was in the clouds
Headed for warm Entebbe
Where he met a smiling immigration officer
Who welcomed him into the country
With a three-month Visitor's visa
Issued in less than five minutes.

II

She was invited to deliver a keynote address
In a Eurozone research institute.

At the embassy where she went to apply for a visa
She was asked to produce a letter of invitation
Specifying why she had to attend a conference so far

And why she, and not any other academic,
Had to present the keynote address.

The letter was scrutinized for irregularities
And several calls were made to the conference convenor
To ascertain that the conference was not ghost
(The consul said he had read of ghost schools and
        hospitals in this country)
And that Professor Bassudde was their keynote giver.

Then came other requirements:
A bank statement she had to produce
Showing how much she earned every month
A letter from her employer
Clearly stating that she was a permanent and
        pensionable member of staff
And a medical certificate
Categorically confirming that she had been vaccinated
        against smallpox
And chickenpox and flupox and fleapox and other poxes
To protect the Eurozone from tropical contagion.

The visa finally came
After fourteen days to-ing and fro-ing the embassy
She travelled to the blessed continent
Where she spent three hours in Passport Control
As officer after officer cross-checked the genuineness
        of this and that –

The blue passport bearing a crested crane and a kob
(With polite requests to her to explain why these two
   creatures
And not any other bird or animal)
The Eurozone visa and the signature it bore
The air ticket (particularly the return date)
The hotel address (room number and telephone contact)
And the programme of the conference
To confirm that Professor Bassudde was indeed a participant.

Tired and sick of these scrutinies
Bassudde headed to the airport the following morning –
Her keynote address safely tucked in her case –
And after securing a seat on the next plane to entebbe
She emailed her apologies to the conference convenors
And showed Europe her backside.

Rush of the Nation

Betty Kaigo

I rush to capture
The rush of the nation
My camera poised
I devour the scene
We want change
One side shouts
No change
The other side asserts

The shepherds stand
In - between
With words like knives
They split the nation
In - between
Themselves
With words sharpened on blades of deceit and paper
Shepherds in the lead
One side shouts
We want change
The other asserts
No change

None, not one is left to sing
For God and my Country
The shepherds feed on the sheep
The sheep scramble for the little grass
Stumbling the nation

Polluting it with slogans
We want change
No change

The Honourable weevil

Samuel Kamugisha

His car, the size of
The deceased's house
Finally screeched to a halt
And out emerged
A huge weevil whose head
Had been swallowed by
A huge mass of fat
And arms mere tree stumps
Thread-bare mourners scrambled
For the honourable handshake
Thin hands swallowed in giant palm.

When the Honourable stood up to speak
Awe reigned
He was sorry, he said
That the deceased died
On a bicycle to the hospital
Only 50km away
Government was too cash-strapped, he mourned
To buy ambulances.
Mourners yawned.

Like a well-fed child, he belched
And gasped and sweated
As he sympathised with people
For the cost of living has pierced
Its way through the roof.

A 20 thousand shillings note
The Honourable fished out
He handed it to the widower
Added a few coins, 'for kids of the Late'

On that note
He asked mourners to
Remember him
In the next election

My Love

Hope Kansiime

Shall I call you my sunshine?
You are NOT violent like its heat,
And I do not have to move outside to feel you.
Sunshine disappears at dusk,
Yet you are my light through day and night.
I shall just call you my love.

Shall I call you my star?
You are brighter and lovelier.
And NOT so far away as the star
The stars disappear at dawn,
Yet you stay with me through night and day
I shall just call you my love.

Shall I call you the beautiful sky?
The inconsistent blue sky?
Sometimes clear, sometimes cloudy and gloomy
Yet you are consistently beautiful,
And never cloudy as the sky,
I shall just call you my love.

Shall I call you a rose?
Your scent is lovelier,
You do not have thorns
And you do not wither like the rose
You are ever beautiful and blossoming
I shall just call you my love

What is It?

Kansiime Hope

What is it?
This, that makes my heart go
Boom......... Boom..........Boom......
Like a drum thumping
Calling upon the villagers for an emergency.
What is this booming........
That makes my heart jittery
To almost a fainting point
When I see you?

What is it?
This, that makes my hands go
Tremble.... tremble.....tremble........
Like dear aged granny...
Trembling, first, the hands,
then quickly spreading like a fire to the whole body,
What is this trembling.........
That makes me go limp
When you touch me?

What is it?
This, that makes my mind go
Blurr..... blurr.....Blurr.....
Like one with amnesia,
trying to recall....but all in vain.
What is this blurring.................
That makes me go blank, that seals my lips

When you whisper in my ear, like a dove cooing?
Tell me , do you ever feel any of these?
What is all this mess you put me in
When you are close by?

Mourn Motherland

Jacob Katumusiime

Mourn motherland
For they have turned you
Into a rag.

For when political giants crash in
This, your arena
You absorb the bloody mess.

And when guns roll in
The neighbourhood
You are rushed
To wipe the bloody mess.

When buffalos lock horns
Scrambling for governance in
Your constituencies
You gulp the bloody mess.

For the many lives
Whose blood you have
Had to rug,
Mourn my motherland mourn.

Mourn
For they have, with a straight face,
Turned you
Into a rag

Lessons Well Learnt (A Poetry Puzzle)

(For Assoc. Prof. Susan Kiguli)

Jacob Katumusiime

For you, woman of strength,
Who rolled up the sleeves
Of my eyes
To the sight of sound verse,
I stretch these vast smiles:

Smiles of gratitude,
Singing you a *may day* song,
Revering your Lineage and
Reassuring you that daily,
I press my poetry beads
Reciting those sacred creeds
You passed on to us:

The Kipling dogma, If,
The Heaney creed, Digging
And daily, replenishing my spirit
With Donne's A Hymn to God the Father
And daily, holding fast to Dreams.

And when my time is come, then shall I test
Nikki Giovanni's guess-
The World Is Not a Pleasant Place to Be,
Careful enough, not to offer
My heart to someone who eats hearts
Careful enough, not to play
Sliding Game-Mutserendende with my life.

And before my son sings for me,
'You are Old Father William',
I will work hard to hear him say
To his friends,
'My Father Is a Simple Man.'
And I, too, will read him My Will
And then, resigned be, to Bellagente's blare,
I Am the Land. I Wait
	And whilst beneath, hope not to ask any being,
	'Ah, Are You Digging on My Grave?'

Fare Thee Well, Kampala

Aloysius Kawooya

Dear Kampala,
You have been a good lover.
You anointed me with your holy oils and indeed I
        smelt good.
We romanced in your parks,
Made love anytime we felt like,
Danced souks in each other's embrace, but that's all
        now gone.
For everything, my dear, I appreciate.
But alas! Dear Kampala,
You were cursed to be beautiful.
And so every man seeks you out.
You have become a polyandrous wife.
You were once fertile, but see what has happened to
        you my dear?
Did you have to spread your legs to every man that
        sought?
Why did you let them suck the life out of your once
        succulent breasts?
The birth control pills, numerous abortions, natural
        calamities have all rendered you barren.
But my darling, am still a young man, with desires
        and fantasies.
I long for children, I need a family and a wife to call mine.
Unfortunately you can give me none.
That's why my dear, I have decided to let you know
        of my new mistress,

Her name is KASESE!
They tell me she is untapped yet ripe,
She knows no abominable ways and she dresses like
a princess.
She was fed on the palm oils from the Congo and
bathes the freshness of the Rwenzori springs.
With her I hope to bear children and raise a family.
Please Kampala, desperate times call for desperate
measures.
I haven't completely forsaken you my love,
I will always come back to you,
For our erotic sessions still keep me awake at night.
Dear Kampala, you will always have my heart!

Broken Souvenir

Aloysius Kawooya

With emotions swarming my whole consciousness
       like bees hurt by a midday fire,
I hold unto memories.
Though they are worn out and dressed in torn feelings.
I still caress the hopes your bitter sweetness created
       in my mind
I still shade pictures of my thoughts of you drawn on
       the virtual canvass you created
I hate to believe that you are no more.
I peddle on the dreams that because of you, faced
       infant mortality.
My eyes now see resentment in a place where colour
       used to play
I hold unto those…… those tangible moods that I
       always hold tenderly in my heart.
Those romantic sights which lived between the twilight and
       the shadow, which made my eyelids feel drunk.
I will no longer hold myself to your make up filled
       promises
But I won't plant the *Luwanyi* tree to draw our
       boundaries.
For you once gave me a life, love.
You once gave me a melody when your tender fingers
       plucked the strings of my *Adungu*!
And you made my heart sound the *Saagala agalamidde*
       rhythm.
Yes, you once made me whole.

Even when you took that person away,
I still have the remains.
Remains that will never make it to any archaeological site.
Remains coated with incense but won't light the driest
        fireplace.
Remains more useless than broken pot fragments,
Yes I will always look to the emptiness of my heart
For you my once loved one,
I will always look at these broken souvenirs

Bloodlines

Gloria Kiconco

My mother is a book
I cannot
read. I do not know:
>How to metaphor the weight of her sorrow
>How many creases she has at the corner of her eyes
>If they crease out of concentration or worry or criticism

The time I massage her back
or legs, she is approachable
but hugs me goodbye
like she hopes not to see me
again
and on the phone sounds
like she is sinking.
So I am not sure

if we should tunnel that water together
or if I should let the current
speak for itself.

It might teach me
how to float.

She also
cannot swim. Some things
mothers cannot
teach their daughters

Some bloodlines were not engineered
to float
and I don't know how to arrange
this fault

Bring us the fallen

Gloria Kiconco

Bring us Icarus.

Lazarus won't do
resurrected in spite of us.

Bring us the fallen
those with misdeeds.

Match our misdemeanors
our simply broken demeanors.

Bring us Daedalus.

Abraham won't do
he fathered righteous sons.

Bring us the forgotten
broken fathers, feathers.

Find us fitting brothers
who've taken selfish measures.

Bring us brothers,
bring us fathers,

broken-hearted families
feather-weight vanities.

Mismatched histories.

Seamstress

Gloria Kiconco

I dreamt of a girl
She lives in a dream
I saw through the surface
not what it seems
Crept by the fine lines
read in between
She seeped through the linen
bled through the seams
Left there a pattern
inkblots and beams
Now I tell her story
It flows out in streams

She, the interpreter of dreams.
She, the Sandman's tongue.
She, the fold at the seams.
She, the expansion of lungs.

This girl sleeps like a story,
every hour a new chapter.
The unraveling of her hair
is the telling of that tale.

Gather around her bed.
Gather inside of her head.
Sacrifice your clarity.
Discard your identity.

Give up all you own.
Once bare, the seed is sown.
You are her, she is you.
Swallow the breath she blew.

What's Native Can't Harm You

Mildred Barya Kiconco

Children of a polished citizen
Visit their grandmother upcountry
Their mother packs tinned foods and waffles
Alternative capsules for vitamins.

They arrive at rural greens
Ripe mangoes and oranges
Waiting for eager hands
The tangerines too have yellowed
The berries are bursting
But mother has warned sternly
Stay off the native.

Grandma urges they relish the gifts in season
They shake their heads.
'Hunger is going to kill you amidst plenty'.
They'll catch a fever if they eat this and that
'What's native never killed nobody',
She's just a bag of old age, they whisper
What can she know?

They open their large bags
Eat high-protein biscuits and chocolates
Swallow capsules
Run around the yard and play and sweat
But turn out stunted like fishermen's hooks.

When We Fall

Mildred Barya Kiconco

Today
I skinned a vulture
And divided the meat
Among us.

Mother
Refused her share
Do you know what vultures feed on?
On us, I said.

We are food
For vulture hovering
Ready to swoop
When we fall.

I Shall Ask Grandma to Write Me a Recommendation

Mildred Barya Kiconco

The scholarship office
States the requirement before admission:
A letter of recommendation from a higher faculty
Familiar with my work;
A tutor, a mentor, who has seen my progress over time
With a smirk on my face
I run to Grandma.

Years gone
We sat under the big eucalyptus tree
Surrounded by pine trees in our compound
She chronicled Histories and Herstories
Dating centuries back

She narrated folk tales
Embedded with morals and vices too
How the kingdom of monsters and humans relate.

The tales she told are the stories I write
The first time I showed the professor my work,
'This can't be you' he bellowed.
'This shows years of practice and genius,
Whose are these?'

I told Grandma who understood it all
'It looks to me your professor is a mediocre', she said.

I shall ask her to write me a recommendation letter
I shall ask Grandma to mail her letter to the
       scholarship office.

The Carcass of Something Hollow & Loud

Melissa Kiguwa

I.
initially, it was only us
squatting on broken glass
like we had no sense, just

prostrations of broken eyes
that could see only ourselves.

alas, there are no wise sensibilities in love,
only the carcass of something hollow & loud.

II.
if there was a fruit, we ate it together.

III.
laughing in a forest rabid with messianic overseers,
a bleating soul trapped lighthouse waiting to see
us fall outside ourselves. but,

we didn't ask to come, to be made from
rib & dust, didn't

ask for free will & a clumsy heart that crashes itself into
tumbling waters of primordial debris.

IV.
initially, there were no wives, no secrets, no
places buried so deep it took waragi & my
fingers to unearth them.

should we have stayed quiet, my love?

stayed hungry, beating our naked chests in
lustful fervor?

V.
i roam outside our homestead, rabid, in heat
holding & letting go these waves of disjointed
        cacophonies.

VI.
i promise to fill the hollow of your rib
with folded innards, soft like dew.

other promises, are falsehoods.

what else do i have to offer while still
licking molasses from my retinas?

VII.
we were casted out into the ring of fire together, &
though i ripped the river's belly while

you wept at a womb torn open,
my love, weren't we leaving eden anyway?

In the Beginning, a Sigh of Darkness

Melissa Kiguwa

in the beginning, there was.

in the expanse between here & beckoning is a sigh of
        darkness, the hallowed bones of eternity.
imagine this universe akimbo with bow legged moons
        huddled in their infinite years of light.

find me when the sun has fallen & we are left before the
        shadows of a beguiling hope, you told
me with a halo of dusk shivering across the brow of your
        tongue. askew, we, searching for our
urchin ways in the crevice of loose skin. instead, sprouting
        mountainous across the railway of forlorn latitudes.

how far we grew, sprouting.

oh, of black holes,
plumes of melancholia,
lips the taste of guava.

oh, of fading skinless into fingers of nomenclature.

on the second day, we howl in a silence that excavates
        marrow from time. imagine ticking shards
of meat cycling each other in lines of perpendicular grief.

the third day layers second upon second, the fourth
        sieves seconds clanging against themselves.

on the fifth day, the time has come to call, to conjure, to
          enter. we growl until our innards ring
sinew. the stream is warm & my face holds like a buoy
          bobbing between your legs. imagine the
sound of a chasm closing into itself; you, the taste of every
          home ever loved.

you bathe me in bones of water, panting into sweating
          orifices dilated open by space collapsing
in on itself. you moan oh na, na, na into the breath of my
          skin until i remember this body, this
layer of fat, its history hot springs of musk.

on the sixth day, we heave our empty stomachs along
          a bank where fish swim weary of drowning
bodies. we survive your fear of drowning by refusing
          metaphors for memories of the blackness
of your skin, a planet of its own. underwater, you hear
          whispers jump from ethers of dust. they
tell you how to trawl your soul from your teeth.

a crown of silver & black, irises about to pop, gills the
          shape of desire.

oh, how your flesh is my flesh.
your legs, mine.
your arms, mine.
your neck, mine.
your moist solitude,
a choking na,

a black na,
a na, na, na full of every home ever loved.

on the seventh day, we rest knowing this is how it
        ends, with the water's bones wedged in the
stream of your moan.

Art of Love

Bob Kisiki

Of a warm July evening
She walked into the gallery
Great pieces everywhere –
Of wood and paper and metal;
Besides her, all else wasn't human
Only imitations:
Of posture, of fashion, of emotion
Here was life; here was no life.

He tapped her on the hand
She flashed a benign grin
And said, 'what say you of this?'
'Not great; not great, I think!'
She faced him straight
And defended Art's cause
'He's the best we've got today,
You've got to admit he is!'

'I admit, and confess I'm he,'
He said and grinned at her.
'Will you pose for a portrait
A memento of our meeting?'
She sat as he took the brush;
And brought her picture to life,
And drove her heart to love
And changed her life for good.

She loved each bit of him
Not just his skilful touch;
He made her sing and laugh
And bless the Lord for him.
He was a god to her;
She was an altar to him,
She would stand by him for life;
Yet he stood for the love of art.

A painter's hand can create
Many forms of life and love;
A lover's eye can keep
One piece that touches her heart;
So while she longed for him –
His art of love; his heart,
He'd found a model to pose
For a newer masterpiece!

Of a chilly December morning
Like a classic piece of art –
She lay alone on the couch
No buyer to name her price!
A great work of art
Only a connoisseur could fathom
By a Connoisseur's hand created
Such is the art of love!

World Poetry Day Special

Bob G. Kisiki

So it is, friend,
A day of poetic expression
Disregarding the drama
of a race that's lost
direction;
Bypassing the prosaic chatter of the masses
as they grumble, their mumbo-jumbo
reverberating through the sky
and hitting back, unheeded;
because the world's used to prose:
Prosaic political prognoses,
pastors preaching peace
in the midst of endemic chaos
marketers making mad money
in shameless prosaic chatter...

So today it is
for the poetic muses
to whisper love
excite hope
mock death
build courage
in strong poetic verses...

today we stand in poetic prowess
to take the world on.

Letter for Resty

Bob G. Kisiki

(To the youngest strange friend I ever had)

It's evening. Grey, heavy clouds, chilly breeze.
Silence all about… Now a mournful bird far off
Laughs… sings… or maybe laments
About this strange and inevitable silence.
The chair you used to prop yourself in is here,
Right in front of me - me, right where I always sat
As we swapped stories and fond accusations. You,
That side of the line, silent, unresponsive.
Yesterday I plucked a flower (here it lies withered)
Off the rose we planted when you were here last;
Its colour is faded, its scent dead, its petals frail.
Yesterday Grace mentioned you - oh, Life!
Called you a gift of nature, a miracle of Humanity…
The silence, Resty! Can't let me concentrate.
But the memory of you makes me warmer -
For all this chill…

The club warrior

Brian Kenneth Kissa

Spring to mind
Something's ingrained in a
       clubber
That innate desire to happen
Under colour drizzles of the
       beaming lights
That dangle upon tipsy lads.
Hundreds keep in audience
To enjoy sets from the finest
       DJs
And yet that's just a mere
       taste
In delights of what's on offer.
He has been given the golden
       disc
As though the champion of
       the orgies festivals
And foolishly staggers back
       home
Neither a penny nor *kaveera*.
       is at hand!
Even the inevitable traffic
       jammers,
Have a certain buzz about
       this leisure sort
Because they are in rush
       hour to see family,

They know those who dump
        themselves,
There, won't even be in position the next day, to clad
In dispensable pairs of under
        wear.

The Namings

Betty Kituyi

When he got his new name,
he had shown patience
at convincing her to come
to a faraway country.

At their arrival,
they slowly lost their sight
as their eyes got used to
a gentle light in the horizon.
They soon found,
they did not need their feet
to keep walking as they began to glide
like birds in a distant sky,
carried by a strong wind.

Surprised yet liking the new way of being,
they desired new names
 - names, like joy,
to describe the wonderful story of this trance.
She felt completely lost
yet tenderly carried by him
who was yet to name her.

He didn't give her a name yet,
what she was becoming
couldn't be named.

The wind softened
and they dropped into a garden
with tender plants of pink and white roses
recognised by delicate petals.
She became clay that could be moulded
into anything he could name.
He made a clay pot out of her
and filled her with honey
which flowed smoothly.

With the honey in his hands,
he had become a bee keeper.
She knew that he didn't recognise himself
and she was the one to name him first.

So he became Wonder.
She echoed his name
in their new world with ancient aura,
King Solomon,
lay with his young maid,
It didn't matter that
he had not given her a name,
she knew she was a poem
being read from Genesis
to Song of Songs.

As she recited this poem to him,
describing how she felt
in this faraway place,
Wow was the name

that formed on his lips.
He said it with such smoothness,
she knew without being told that,
that was the name he had finally given her.

With new names,
they both knew they were in
a sacred place in the garden.
What could be felt and said was all they were.
He had found a special key
to her heart as only a few men can
to a heart of a woman.

Forgive to Remember

Betty Kituyi

I will remember
How in that moment
I chose to gather
The scared child within
Whose world
Was burning with fires,
Real flames that engulfed
The threads of her favourite wrapping,
a woman's wrapping
drawn in figures
Of sun,
now lay in flakes of
grey ash.

To forgive is
to remember
How I sank together
With the ashes
of my burnt feelings,
Ash and dust
Adding colour and substance
to an internal
Stream whose depth
I knew not.

To forgive,
I will remember

that I curled
My foam to sleep
On a cold lonely night
And woke up
To find
my unburnt spirit
Waiting to be encouraged
To carry on the day
that had
Already began.

To forgive I will
Remember that I had
To forgive myself
And forgive
the being
that had reduced
My bright covers
To grey ashes.

To forgive,
I will remember.

Cloud Escape

Betty Kituyi

What would happen to my view
if I let the clouds roll on each other in their moods?

What would happen
if I let then form dragons gods
in their formless flow?

If the gods were to build my house?
Would I sleep on tree tops
and watch the world drift by
like a giant ship on this trip we call life?

And what have we done to our world?
Have we created to free ourselves?
Or created to confine us in our limitedness?

What if in this limited place
of terror and ugliness,
I chose to find habitation in the clouds
where I can be bounced from one cloud to another
like trampoline jumps
when I chose to tease myself
out of that settled boredom.

Will I stretch and roll?
Will freedom become mine
to stretch like a hunter with his spear?

Will the savannahs shift to the skies
If mine is to let go?

How about dance?
Do I need feet to dance
on the carpeted canopies of time?
Will angels become my dance partners?
or eagles my guides to higher skies?

And who is blocking my world view?
Is it the sky scrapers
or myself choosing to stare at mud floats
or rubbish dumps?

Like cirrus,
why choose to be condensed
when I can stretch to conquer the skies?

The Rally
George Kiwanuka

I braved the scorching sun
squeezing through the cocktails of folks and lads
my mission was simple and pure
To violently plead for an explanation
From the loud demagogue at the podium
demanding why five years down the road
He's returned to bask in the same unfulfilled
        promises as last

Silently praying for answers
My thirst to mete judgement was unquenchable-insatiable
Looking at his lifeless eyes I planned to question
about the wax that had sealed his ears from hearing the
        dying hungry cries during his tenure
I failed to decipher his eyes from his heart and mind
Immune to our wails yesterday, today he sang promises
        of self sacrifice

He was the promised son, he said…the long awaited
        messiah
Better schools, medicine in hospitals, better pay, even
        flawless *kolansi* roads
As I hungered for signs of shame from him, his oblivious
        'absence' hit me
his body was there, but 'he' was in another realm
A realm whose realization this rally would determine
like a sledge hammer, his fate depended on our gullibility

In this realm, wads of cash awaited him
Hectares of vast land, palatial mansions and gold
Fat voluptuous women sighed his name,
Herds of cattle and sheep, tractors on virgin land
In that realm the poor riff-raff who made the electorate
          had no place

I felt his fan of lies swell up and grow
Like a monster feeding off our fear, desperation and hope
His deceit cast a large shadow over the multitudes
          that had
Like blind sheep gathered ceremoniously
The shadow like the wings of a large ignorance, disease
          and death-carrying bird blinded us

Then, as if in a drunken stupor
I was too weak to turn away from the tempting gaze
the seductive feel of secret sin
Facing the ground I bowed in shame
as I held out my hand to take his bribe

A Mogul's Epitaph

George Kiwanuka

I stared into the cold chapel across the casket
Caught glimpse of my lifeless body
lying still in that huge varnished wooden prison
seemingly floating in a sea of hypocritical wreathes
all my power and millions irrelevant

From a distance, bewilderment served me her blows
At the few people who sincerely mourned me
I saw the futile efforts to feign grief
They tried to lie, in vain, but their grins gave them away
Deception ruled, they concocted good inexistent
        memories of me

I saw them all scheming for the vast property and
        legacy I had left
I scoffed at this, the cut throat politics I had taught
        them would be the death of them
I saw my family infiltrated, contaminated by greed
My wives, raised to be sisters, plotting each other's
        demise
My sons laying it bare in air tight bloody war, their
        sisters picking sides
A preference to spill their own blood to divide the dirty
        wad of cash I had left
like spoils and booty from a conquest war

At the far end of the chapel
I caught sight of Makumbi, my scribe friend from the paper
His face was expressionless as he drew his claws
Laying his traps like a fisherman's net with hopes for a
        story about me
Prodding my partner's and acquaintances for dirt,
        net-worth stories do not sell he says
When all this plastic grief melts away, my life will be a lesson

Regret After Danger

Sonia Koheirwe

The happy moments I had
Now gone
The smiles I saw
Now ceased

The memories I shared
The stories I told
The potentials I had
All came to an end

I regret
The choice I made
I was blind like a toe
Hitting stones everybody could see

At this age
I have known to wear many faces
I have known to carry things in my palm
And not feel the weight.

Ugliness

Juliet Kushaba

In the gutters
Stand enormous heaps
of garbage,
long-forgotten:
rotten tomatoes,
rotten water-melons,
left-over food
buttered bread,
vegetables…
All maggots,
dull and dark
like dog waste
that has been exposed
to rain and sun.
The smell
flows around
pierces its way
through the air
into the nostrils
of the city

70 Plus

[Tribute to my late Dad]
Alice Tumwesigye Kyobutungi

It has no medicine
And no cure
It knows no difference
Or variety
People are just figures
Faces mere silhouettes
As for the food,
It all tastes the same
And the hours are all alike
Night and day all merge into
One long endless night
In this life whose salt has dissolved
Whose light has waned
Into a murky opaque void.

The Don.

Alice Tumwesigye Kyobutungi

In a strange land
Among foreigners
You quietly forged a way
Of blending…

In sure conviction
You certainly trusted
Your acumen
To win the souls
And warm the way
For a penny in hand
In a strange land.

Classless

Alice Tumwesigye Kyobutungi

They own it all
Who own nothing
Like the beetle
That buzzes around the flowers
Claiming them all…
They lack it all
Who lack nothing
For abundance is
The enemy of appreciation
Like the complacent native
Whose hive is taken
Right before his eyes.

Our perfume

Steven Lubangakene

My mother was a flower
Bearing fruits that we became
But when a flower matures
It withers.

That's how it was
In my father's compound,
The only flower withered

She was our sunrise
The perfume that kept us close
But the bottle broke
And gave birth to Bitterness
Gave birth to Sorrow and Pain
they became our sisters and brothers

Rest in peace beauty flower
Father too still weeps wells of tears
That can't be held in the broken pieces of the bottle.

Do Not Rejoice

Susan Malinga

They are in a well-lit room
Eating, chatting, laughing
Without a care
Suddenly, someone switches off the light!
Darkness, confusion, pain!
For a long time, till they give up.
Then;

He switches on the light
Everybody rejoices with him.

The darkness, confusion and pain disappear
It's back to eating, chatting and laughing
It does not last long though
Suddenly, someone switches off the light!
A candle is improvised
Little activity goes on.
Then;

He switches on the light
Everybody rejoices with him.

They put out the candle
It is back to the usual
Activity increases, plans are made
Suddenly, someone switches off the light!
A candle is improvised

Activity continues regardless.
Then;

He switches on the light
Nobody rejoices with him.

Nobody puts out the candle
Activity continues as it were
Both the candle and the light stay on
They plot to expel the suspect
Their anger is simmering
Nobody switched off the light again!

Behind the Teeth

Solomon Manzi

Do motes of dust
Remember the stone –
Whence they came?

Does each raindrop
Recall the cloud –
From which it fell?

Must we invent smiles
For every flashing lens?
As if afraid –
To share our pain with history.

Must the mirror –
By us be judged;
As if what we see inside
Is born, on her other side?

Do laughter and anger –
Sit behind the teeth?
Lying side by side
In the folds of the tongue;
Casting lots –
On who will be summoned first?

Does wisdom hang –
From the roof of the mouth?
Staff in hand –

Gently knocking
Against that door
Of locked white stones

That grows south?
Are joy and silent hope
Seated back/ to back
Beneath darkening gums
Cuffed, and roped in mirthless chain?

Do lore and myth
Peep out –
From between the teeth?
As two chaste maids
Loath –
Of our tendency to waste words?
Of we
their unremembering kin and kith?

Kaisiki, take me to Kyoga

Solomon Manzi

Kaisiki,
Take me to Kyoga –
Where the white egret screams
As if in this life, she shan't longer stay;
Where the grey waters crash, against the rocky land
In foamy waves, high, as tidal streams;
Embracing by heart and hand –
The lost loves, of their dreams.

Take me to Kyoga –
In whose mild, swishing shallows
The naked infant doth play;
Chanting rhymes, at the overhead, gliding swallows;
As the wary mother, knitting straw baskets
Upon the golden sands –
Watches, with short breath and long sigh.

Take me to Kyoga,
Where the striving fisherman;
Before dawn doth wake –
Praying to the god of lake
To keep the wild storm at bay;
And his boat, from heave and tremulous sway.

Kaisiki, take me to Kyoga –
Where the soul, of this old land
Forever dwells;

And the spirit, of this open sky
Endlessly swells.

Where the fishes in the water
In joyous circles swim;
And the trees upon the shore
With native grace swing;
As the little birds in their boughs
With soft chirrup, do sing.

Where the misty palm –
Of black night descends;
And the restless waters grow calm
Beckoning us
To their vast, liquid ends.

Kaisiki –
Blow on – gentle, gentle wind
Glow on – my soft, soft pearl
And take me to Kyoga.

From the very beginning –
Teach me these things, again.

If death must court me

Solomon Manzi

If death must court me –
Let him come, at the beginning of counting
When words were young and still learning to speak
– and the eyes of time, had lost not their callow
glimmer.
Let him rouse me from the dream of age
In which men shrivel up and forget to wake
As forming streams tire, of riverward journeys
– and give up the fight.

May he find me curled up, in the womb of a tulip
Where innocence and wonder make their home
And yoke in the night, to conceive things pure and warm.

May I be found reading a poem, in the mouth of a lily
Where raindrops stop to rest, and for a while tarry
– catching their breath, on their way to the sea.

Where dewdrops flee in the yawning dawn
To shelter from the stirring sun –
As baby leaves scamper off to school
To learn greenness, from browning elders.

Let him come to me, festooned in shy flowers
Wearing a laurel of broken clouds
And there, ask for my hand.

Loving you, has made me soft

Dear one –
I am grown soft, from loving you
As old stone/ melting
Under the abiding affections of the sun
Or the blushing petal/ shrinking

At the butterfly's frisky touch.

Your wooden wand –
Cloaks me over, in supple skin//
I give way
Under your enduring kisses/
Warm night, upon warm night.

Aye –
Yours/
Is an everyday magic –
Visible. Touchable. Undying.

I feel, those things felt
By a wet morning soil
Gently stroked
Under the light tread/ of the loping cat
Or the mellowed leather
Of a boy's mud-spattered shoe
Enamored –
Of his small, familiar feet.

It softens me, Akullo
This loving of yours –
Winds me up in the tight twists
Of your dark, spiral hair.

I am not myself, longer-more/ no
But neither are you, beloved –
We long past, became
This knot of oneness.

Recresting the Crane

Solomon Manzi

The wide-winged bird of our old land, has fallen to the
       ground;
And the trembling sky has threatened, upon us to
       tumble down –
With a deep sound.

The long-legged crane of our ancient home, in the wild
       does roam;
And the place, she once came from –
Is cold as ice, and no more warm.

We ask ourselves –
Who shall recrest our crane?

The crackling fires, round which we once gathered
Have vanished before our very eyes, like a child dying
       before a parent –
As if before our tears they have cowered;
And the songs of the night have gone silent –
As if of our faithless ears, they have tired.

Of the music-less darkness they leave behind,
We ask –
Who shall recrest our crane?

Who shall recover her nest, and hatch her fragile,
       speckled eggs?

Those round brittle gems, which glow, like the inside
of a dream –
Now float motherless, upon the marshy stream.

Who shall shelter her, from the stormy weathers?
And smooth out her tousled feathers;
That have grown dull with neglect –
In these loveless heathers?

Who shall return to her –
Her jet, her crimson, her sunshine
Without which, her soul has become a colourless shadow;
And her heart weeps, in endless sorrow.

Who shall recrest our crane?

Who shall crown her with a golden plume –
And gown her, upon a silver loom;
Who shall teach her again, to saunter –
With a royal swagger?

Shall she be raised, once more, above this deafening roar?
Shall she rise, above the great Nile, and soar?

Who shall find her lost old nestlings, and stray newest
brood –
And in her, rekindle the joy of motherhood;
As a flame that burns upon life's own wood –
For now, and for good.

Equilibrium

Kahirwa Mbabazi

"…it must be pink, you're a girl!
Drop the robot, here's your Barbie doll.
Plait her hair, stay away from football.
Paint your lips, show your hips.
A longer dress. Don't be a slut.
Still, lie 'I'm no virgin. Anything but!'

Where's your diamond? You're a girl!
Hurry to graduate from college school,
it's high time marriage became cool.
The children must be healthy and walking
before the clock stops ticking.
Remember, be a parent in the playroom
and a player in the boardroom.
A professional in the cooking room
and a pornstar in the bedroom…"

To find peace in all this insanity,
to scream silently and peacefully conquer,
is to dance in the very poetry of womanhood.

Life Without You.

Praise Mugisha

Picking up the tattered pieces
That from my heart have fallen,
Every piece holds a memory
Bringing a smile to my face
And a hardened tear in my eye
Filled with pride
Filled with pain
Of what used to be
Now fallen
Like petals from a red rose
Whose scent I still smell
In promises unfulfilled
in the shadow of your walking away
In the knowledge that we share.
In the tomorrow without you

I Saw the Typhoon...

Bernard Mujuni

Early in the morning,
I heard someone groaning,
Amidst the heavy down pour
Of the heavenly strong winds that roared,
Followed by an ear-splitting thunder that raged..

I SAW THE TYPHOON…

I threw my hollow-pillow by the windy window
And saw in the middle,
Of the road, a man with a blown fiddle,
His little dog whimped and whimped
And ran across the road like a toad,
In the Middle of the road

I SAW THE TYPHOON...

I reached by my side, the umbrella,
And braved the weather,
Like a bird without feathers,
amidst the gusty weather

I SAW THE TYPHOON…

I moved my feet with stagger,
As though I had swagger,
My breath, was a struggle;
Eyes, littered with water,

Blown far by the weather,
A man, across wailed, like on the cross,
And thought death but never...

I SAW THE TYPHOON...

A woman and the child gasped,
For mother air,
As though she had no hair,
With the wind blowing the umbrella....
The boy with a kite, on the bike,
tried a hike,
But like a flight, was swept aside,
By the might of the tide.

I SAW THE TYPHOON...

The trees, gathered in sombre stature,
Structures and bridges buttressed and battered
Train station, without trace of some train, but rain
The grey clouds, up in the air,
Grew in strength and measure,
As floods, ran the floor,
Like none was to care for air and weather

I SAW THE TYPHOON...

The Little White Kid in December of 1984

Beverley Nsengiyunva Nambozo

In December 1984, a little white kid
Threw snow at my dad's car.
And then he just laughed-
He clutched his stomach
And his shoulders shook.

When I saw the snow
Around his feet melting,
I knew he was pissing on himself.

Oy!
Buzz Off!

   He echoed me.
Oy!
Buzz Off!

And we stood facing each other
The snow covering his piss.
The snow falling on my eye-lashes.

Oy!
Buzz Off!

   His echo came softer this time.
Oy!
Buzz Off!

Purley Avenue in December of 1984.

We were once Young

Rashida Namulondo

We were once young
The world we once ruled.
We somersaulted over drum kits
Set fire on the bass guitar.

Our feet stamped chords
That caressed Mother Nature
Making her rethink her future.

Through the microphone
We fed them on our youthful energy.
Giving birth to hope,
Resolving the yesterdays,
Kissing the tomorrows.

We were once young
A thousand souls singing our dreams
In unison.
Our melody spread out to the skies.
We burned the floor,
Ripped the drums,
Applause.
Lights dimmed.
Curtains down.

We were once young
Our zeal opened the doors for today.

Teach Me

Rashida Namulondo

Teach me how to write
How to express pain
Piercing through my body
Dripping with salty red waters.
How to put a face to a hollow emptiness
Like a drying crater lake
Dry of life
But living.

Show me
How to put metaphors
For the depth of my soul's grief
Words that put kindness to it
So I can paint hope to the new generation.
Words that put skin
To my imprudence and prejudice
Justifying me
As an fair minded person.

Take a good look at my shame
Paint it heartlessly
Put no colour of comfort.
Please guide my hand
Help me paste my fear,
On paper for a world to see.

Teach me expression
For those that come after me to find
And through their eyes
My emotions shall live on.

On her grave.

Rashida Namulondo

On my mother's grave I wept
My soul bled
For a woman
Who had fought cultural bondages
And rose to her feet
To rebuild her reality
Amidst the storms of new and old.
      On her grave I bid farewell
To a heroine
Whose charisma
To learn the new ways
Yet keep the olden ways
In practice
Taught me to be true
      I wept for a friend
      A lover
      A sister
      A revolutionist
Who turned her house into a battle field
'All women shall rise
A day to come'
She said.
      I wept for a friend
      A teammate
      A symbol of new embracing old
I wept for a mother gone too soon.

Mother's struggles

Agness Namusisi

I want to thank you mother
For I know I sucked you dry
Your bones could be counted from your skin
Because you could not deny me you.

In hospital you stuck with me
Others abandoned the terrible smell I gave off
I remember somebody saying;
"The owner of the dead body touches the rotting part."

I remember how you fed us mother,
For 10 years,
Without a job
Without a husband
You became the family head and feet
We were the poorest, mother
Even a dog could not pass our compound
Because we took years without ever cooking meat.

We ate salted water and maize meal
We sipped sugarless maize porridge
But life was not desperate at all.
You kept us happy, mother
Sometimes strangers shared the little we had,
They paid us laughter.

I do not know how much I can thank you
Even if I worked for a thousand years
And gathered all my pay in a basket
I would never raise enough to pay you back
Because mother, you never put a price tag to your toil.

Irresponsible Husband.

Mercy Aweko Nimungu

Thin, like a walking stick,
His tongue dark like smoked meat,
Teeth yellow like a hurricane lamp
From severe smoking.

You stagger like ajono in a troubled pot
No idea of the direction of your home
Vomit and mucus stained
What an irresponsible husband.

By luck you reach home
You ask for food you have not provided
You beat your wife and children like you don't know
them
You spit foolish and helpless on them.

Watch out though
Before your words become you.
Retrace your steps
Before ajono pot swallows you up.

Kaleidoscope!

Jason Sabiiti Ntaro

You see,
Africa is not about negativity,
Or about black slavery or kids working in industries.
Africa isn't only about blood spilled by tyrants,
Wars ran by children, or AIDS and frustration.
Africa isn't about black being beauty,
About women with heavy booty,
Or green grass and sky scraping hills.

Africa is about Africa!

Africa isn't about natives walking about naked,
Or about corrupt leaders leaving us frustrated.
Africa isn't about land mines and illegal arms,
Or rebels leaving us all alarmed...state of panic.
Africa isn't about Africans battling malnutrition,
Or politicians with verbal constipation.
Africa isn't about children befriending dirt and disease.
Or about being comfortable with dis-ease!

Africa is about Africa!

Africa is about the individual, that solitary soul...
Not those diamond rocks or gold!
Sure we have minerals,
Sure we got beautiful natural blessings...
But there's something bigger than that that you are missing.

As opposed to the talk of nature, I speak of natives.
Of that hand crafted beauty named...people.
People of warm hearts, people with kind smiles,
And nights wild.

And when I say wild I don't mean forest jungle wild.
I mean the fire that burns within souls of men, of women,
and of children.
The fire that moves them from yesterday,
to today, and tomorrow.

So smile my African friend.
But do not smile for Africa,
No,
Smile about Africa.

We watch her.

From birth she was sang a song long gone silent
Where voice and word were not bed separate.
Where life was not a tablet
Upon which rule is fact.

A world where spirit is the back of bone.
Where kindness is the norm.
And where the heart and not brain is start.
But the world that life feeds her,
 Leads her to question where her leaders lead her.
All the splendour and bright colour surrounds her,
Bright lights blind her,

Bind her,
Blind her from seeing herself.

Now like a puppet on a shelf,
She dances to the tunes her stringed shackles twing
        and twang.
She is no longer human.

Clueless she searches for a way back home.
Questions like waves crash, but she stands alone.
The elders have left her, to the devices of the vultures.
Who poke at her eyes, until her spirit slowly dies.

And we watch her!

We watch her with our arms crossed hiding our hearts.
We feed our lusts ignoring our part.
We wade in the muck of a selfish world stuck.
We close our lazy eyes, and lean on luck!

We have poisoned our veins with blood of deceit,
Our nature is fading, our wants consume our needs.
We stab at our core, the soul,
It bleeds.
We are faded and empty,
No nature in our feet!

So we suffer our children our past misdeeds.
The seeds of deceit we plant, they reap.
We wage our wars on innocent civilians,
Neglecting our heritage, sipping on foreign provisions.

We taint our own skin eye-lining the divisions,
THIS REVOUTION NEEDS REVISION...
Poisoned leaders **MUST** no longer make decisions,
This is our land, our home, our definition!

I Don't Want To Know

Joel Benjamin Ntwatwa

I don't want to know about you,
About those boys you talk with, on your phone,
Or the girls,
The ones you flash your heart to, and they laugh and
          you laugh,
The ones you like to try and taste
The ones who come and leave
Empty tins, rolling stones
While I sit here waiting for you
Gathering moss,
Those running waters pouring where everyone pours
As I quietly wait, running deep for your soul.

I don't want to know.

You're piercing my midnight thoughts
While you and your boys, and girls
Exchange morning thoughts each time you meet.
You're the sack I poured into
Which had holes,
The shoes I sought to fill
Which had no soles.

I loved you deliberately
Yours was whenever you felt like it
So perhaps I don't want to know how you are
And I'm okay with it.

But am I okay with it?
This bittersweet when you leave
And come back when you like
A revolving door in your life
Always walking in and out.

I despise the feelings I've grown since I met you.
They neither heal
Nor completely destroy
I'm a walking effigy
In love with you.

Can I not be a thing?

Calvin Ocitti

Can I not be a thing?
Humans must know
The world is not flat
The world is round
Life is not straight
Life is round
We are here not forever
We are here only for a season
And seasons go round

But if beyond everything there is nothing
Then God knows nothing of things beyond
Then everything is everything
And everything is nothing
But first something must decide that things are things
For without something to say things are things
Tell me how something would be something

But if something is nothing
Then nothing is known by a thing
So the thing that says something is nothing makes
        something a thing
If Femrite says you and I are writers
Then we are something
Then you and I are things
Otherwise nothing would have been known by
        things about you and I

Can you not be
Be that something before the morning grows out of
          your hands?
Yes we can because we are things and we are night
and
          we are light and
we are dark and we are one
And I am the warrior I am the writer I am the dream boy
I am a sign of change for our nation for a bright writing
          future.

Afro-Democracy

Julius Ocwinyo

I know little Inglis
But I hear
In BBC
In Voice of Amerika
In Radio German'
Dey all say: 'Democracy'.

I read newspaper
Dey all say: 'Democracy'.
Dey all say
Democracy mean
Multi-party.
Dey all use
Big word
Long word
Difficult word
Word dat I look in Michael West
And not find dere
Word dat confuse my head!

White man come
            and go
Multi-party come
            and disappear
Umbrella party come
            and vanis'
No-party come
            and pass, too

But I not get money
For my children
To go good school
I not get money
For my wife to buy
Beautiful *gomesi*
I not get money
To buy s'irt
For my back
Or trouser
For my backside
(Dat 'backside' I learn from Amerikan doctor).

De crops I grow
Maize
     and simsim
Millet
   - and banana
Pineapple
     and bean
Coffee
     and cotton,
Dey buy dem cheap
Like yam
As I eat cassava
And pumpkin-leaf.

I open my mout'
And somebody kick me
In buttock;

I say somet'ing
And somebody knock me
On head.
Yet dey all talk
Of democracy
Yes, dey all do.

I don' care
About multi-party
Or single party
Or army party
Or umbrella party
Or no-party.
I need ox-plough
Not *jembe*
I need power saw
Not panga
I need you buy
My crops
Expensive.

I need protekson:
No-one kill me
 In de day
Or in de night.
Give me dese t'ings
And I will vote you
I swear I will!

Okello's Gripe

Julius Ocwinyo

I know, old woman
I *do* know
Your husband.
You've bugled
His greatness
At meetings
And in church.
Humble, too, he was
The climb, too,
He found hard
Like I do,
I believe.

You came along
Didn't you?
With eyes dazzled
No?
Espied the cattle
You did
And the cash
With eyes rapt
      starved
       rapacious,
Your heart craving
Easy fulfillment.

You went up,
Shirt-tail passenger,
Up and up:
>   His past unreminisced
>   His poverty unacknowledged;
Your eyes avaricious
Calculating
By current rustic splendour blinded.

Poor, too, he was
Old woman
The climb, too,
He found hard
That much
I *do* know!

The AIDS Virus

Lawrance Max Odongo

My name is Aids
And I am proud of it
Because I am the most feared virus on earth.

I am still young and powerful
Born only thirty years ago
A descendant of a union
Between man and monkey in Congo

I am a scientist because I live in
A human body and
Work there against human scientists.

The doctor works hard to get rid of me
But I work harder to establish myself
And get rid of him

I am a religious catalyst
Because I speed up people's journey to God
So they accept God more because of me
When they realise that they have acquired me.

I save the children from being eaten up
By this greedy world
So I kill them while they are still young.

I do not discriminate.
I kill doctors, lawyers and teachers,

I kill Reverends, blacks, yellows, reds and all.
My victims range from unborn to oldest.

I am champion.
Presently I hold world's number one killer record.
I love the position.
You might want to be careful about me!

Death

Francis Peko Ogaku

Death, so threatening a word!
Snatching like an hawk
Selectively and indiscriminately
Showering us with absurdity.

I delve for your cognisance
Gorgeous figure of fragrance?
My heart raging with lumping temporariness
For your calamitous coeval with happiness
Nullifying us deleteriously
Astounding us with your cupidity
The alacrity for our breath
Snatching the breath God gave us- God?
Leaving us deflated of the sap of life
Devoiding us of delectation.

Death,
Do you connive with God,
To see man descend to useless demise?
You and God in connivance
Faded memories of those days of Noah
The days of God's loud whispers to man
Gone are those days of manna

God in his abode of comfort
Twiddling his majestic beards
Unburdened by man's plights

Unfeeling to man's agony
Deeply against man's delectation
Brandishing his authentic teeth
As man perish toiling
Sweating in obedience to his ultimatum

Death,
You are a good pal
I have learnt your thefty savages
Experienced you both with soul and body
I don't shiver at your mention
But for God,
Not an inch of experience
God, you are tired – retire!!!

Death
Take me not in my sleep
You gluttonous parasite dwelling in me
Your uncomplaining host
Take me; willing for denudation
The host dies with the parasite
I will conquer you when I die
Let me die
Just let me die, oh death!!!

The Debate is the Thing

James Ogoola

The Debate is the Thing:
Candidates decked in a gorgeous rainbow of colours
      speaking the speech of rhetoric
      dissecting the discourse of oratory
      displaying the skills of eloquence
      the politics of persuasion –
      All ready to compete in the ideal marketplace of ideas.

The Debate is the Thing:
Electors tuned on the ear, intent to listen
Viewers with sharp hawk's eye
      keenly scouring the TV screen
All sitting on Solomon's seat:
      to judge the agile from the docile
      to gauge the nimble from the feeble
      to assess the adept from the inept;
      to weigh the analytical from the anecdotal:
      Thereby to distil the winner from the loser.

The Debate is the Thing:
Here, no cheap drama of the ordinary political rally
Here, no base speech of the idle or the vulgar
      no shrill tongue of demagoguery
      no sly politics of the empty pledge or the
            hollow promise,
Here, only the nobler ideas and ideals of the mind
      take pride of place :

ready to edify the collective soul of the Electorate;
eager to quench the political thirst of the Nation.

On the campaign trail:
candidates stand on the shifting sands of vain populism
At the Debate the candidates stand on the solid platform
of cardinal principles and critical policies –
With firm figures and fine facts, they wow the audience.
With startling wit and stunning humour, they charm
the Electorate –
The Debate soothes the rancour of political nastiness;
it binds the wounds of partisan pettiness.

Truly, the Debate is the Thing!

15 January 2016
Imperial Royale Hotel, Room 808, Kampala, Uganda.
DEDICATED to the First ever Presidential Electoral Debate
in Uganda, (held at the Serena International Conference
Centre, Kampala, on 15 January 2016) comprising Presidential
Candidates: Dr. Abed Bwanika; Maj. Gen. Benon Biraaro;
Col. Dr. Kizza Besigye; Eng. Elton Joseph Mabiriizi; Rt.
Hon. Amama Mbabazi; Dr. Maureen Kyalya Waluube; Prof.
Venansius Baryamureeba – with incumbent President Yoweri
Kaguta Museveni *in absentia*. Without a doubt, this: "The
Debate of the Jubilee", changed the course of the electoral
history of the Country; and bent the curve of the electoral
platform of the Nation.

Bricks, Bullets & Brains

[Death by Any Other Name]

James Ogoola

To die, wearied down
> weighed low with a deadly load of bricks
> in a forced labour camp
> building mammoth monuments to Nazi pomp?

Or, to succumb as a hapless prisoner of war
> shot point blank thru' the heart
> by a bullet of the sadistic soldier
> Guarding the grim gate
> of a death camp?

Or, perhaps, to sniff the poisoned plume
> of the toxic fumes
> wafting thick and heavy from
> the ghastly gas chamber?

But then, lest we forget: there always were
> other equally fanciful alternatives:

For one: to fry dry as a cheap chicken fry
> charred to dark ashes in the white hot furnace
> of the furious fuehrer of Auschwitz and Dachau;
> > Belligerent butcher of Birkenau —
> meantime, yielding the precious golden tooth
> > in your dead jaw
> to the gluttony of the greedy executioner !

Or, perhaps, even more gripping:
> to have your brain chilled alive in your skull;

frozen into a ball of ice-cold brain yoghurt
in a laboratory experiment
executed by the wicked witches of the war?

Behold then, the fine array of choices.
One could never die for lack of a choice
writ large on Hitler's Choice- Menu offering :
Bricks, Bullets and Brains!

25 April, 2014
Documentation Centre Museum, Nuremberg   ,
Germany

DEDICATED as a minute monument to the memory of
the Millions dead; who perished like worthless fleas,
dying horrific deaths in the terrible death traps of Hitler's
horribly hideous War of 1939-1945.

A Floral Birthday
[A fragrant Greeting to Flogola]
James Ogoola

A flower is a beauteous bride indeed.
Her smile, is superbly sensational.
Her scent, is perfume for the Royals
Her form, is the epitome of gorgeous magnificence.

Sweeter than the sweetest honey, is her nectar.
sweeter than the sweetest honey.
The texture and fabric of her coloured gown
       is superior by far to the ravishing rainbow.
Her composure forms the very essence
       of graceful elegance.
The petals of each single flower, are a holy temple
Filled with a fabulous bouquet of fragrant incense.

A flower is a sweet sanctuary to the busy buzzing bee;
       a perfumed playground to the majestic butterfly:
       (Fashion Queen of the insect kingdom —
       gracefully floating on the wings of a
            refreshing breeze
       decked in her mystic coat of complex colours)
The moth, the beetle and all long-lipped kindred kith and kin
       are perennial pilgrims to the floral shrine.
They all stream to the living fountainhead
       for a drink of holy honey
       in exchange for a load of golden pollen.

Surely, of all the seasons of the year,
> Spring is the authentic reason for floral exuberance.

This, the season for the flower in ecstasy:
> the reason for every bush and shrub to blossom,

the season for every blossom to explode into bloom
the reason for every bloom to paint
> dim sadness of Winter
> into the radiant gladness of Spring.

The gentle rain of Spring;
the mild temperature of its warmth;
the malleable soil of the season
> rich in the manifold manure of Autumn and Winter—

combine in Nature's miracle cycle of life.
Collectively, they concoct the perfect cocktail
> needed for the floral midwifery
> that gives birth to the bouncing baby flower!

What then is a flower to the world?
Of what value is floral bliss:
> beyond sensual appeal to visual pleasure?

The flower speaks, not to the eye, but to the heart.
She grips, not mere sight, but inner insight.
She lends a sparkle to the soul;
> and sends a smile to all.

She turns a melancholy world of the lonely
> into the merry warmth of the lovely.

Floral beauty that we behold:
> beautifies our brow;
> beatifies our spirit!

And so, darling Florence—
        tropical flower of florescence
You are, for all time flavour
Surpassing by far every flower
        of a single season or day.

Happy Birthday today!

        8th June 2012
A BIRTHDAY gift to Florence Nightingale Wandera Ogoola,
beauteous bride of enduring flavour!

Moonrise

James Ogoola

The stars come out to bask in the mystical glow
      of their mesmerizing lights.
They come to join the royal parade of the Matriarch
      of the Skies.
Smiling a gleaming smile, wearing a captivating grin –
      the ornate Princess of Poise shows her radiant face
      on the distant horizon.
She emerges above the Dome of the lofty Firmament,
      to begin her enchanting nocturnal catwalk
          through a galaxy of glittering lights.

Daintily, she picks her delicate way
      through the airy terrain above.
Majestically, she inclines her magnificent face
      to the admiring millions below.
Seductively, she blows a hypnotizing kiss
      to the adoring host of the twinkling stars;
      which reverently kindle the vast skies
      to illuminate her milky highway.

Discreetly, she reveals only one quarter of her noble face-
      to unmask the abounding beauty of her
          crescent smile.
Gradually, she unveils one whole half of her beaming brow-
      to expose the glitter of her sparkling countenance
Eventually, mask, veil, skirt and gown she drops altogether
      to lay bare the resplendent radiance of her entire body:

a body befitting the luminous Queen of the
     Celestial Lights!

Hers, is a mystic body of deep mythology:
   bewitching to the amorous lovers;
   beguiling to the sky-gazing astronomers;
   bedazzling the space-chasing astronauts:
   bestirring blustery storms on the high seas:
   befuddling the memory and twisting the mind
   of tough-minded mariners !

Behold then, the sterling splendour of the Moonrise
   which paints a fluorescent firelight
     on the dark canvass
     of the dim gloomy night!

  21 August, 2009

Foetal Position
[Sex Slave at Ten]
James Ogoola

She was hardly Ten,
      still shy of a Teen.
She was dragged, shrieking, into hard adult sex:
Her own father lying on top of her chest
      grunting contentedly: all grotesque!
There, in the dark outback of their squalid tin ghetto
      a father gruesomely desecrated his own baby's
          virgin flower!
        not once, not twice: but serially, over
          unending time:
        all covered up under the sly shroud of silence!

She was barely beyond Ten
      he was trapped and tricked into the human
          traffic lanes-
      plane-loaded by her own family,
      transported to a destiny of treachery
      to a distant land of modern slavery.
There, her first master forced himself onto her
      in the full glare of TV's dirty pornography
Drilling through her tender innocence:
      grunting ghastly groans astride her frail baby body;
      right there: atop a freezing bed board –
      where she lay frigid, terrified, and curled up:
        like a foetus!

She, a vulnerable child of wicked trafficking in
human cargo,
was shipped abroad for the tantalizing lure of a
job and a school –
The fickle lure turned, instead, into a desert
mirage of vile servanthood.
She was caged and detained; like a beast,
to slave away
in the misery and loneliness of a hostile
cell of sexual bondage:
confined three thousand lonesome miles from home!

She was left limp and motionless: hushed down:
unable to speak up -
lying chained in emotional comma.
As she turned Eleven,
she was left prematurely but permanently wounded:
writhing and wallowing in a frightful pool of
psychological trauma –
shrunk for ever in youthful deformity
for ever curled up:
like a foetus!

After the one hundredth attack: of mutilation and
molestation
the child thrust her bruised soul and battered body of
exploitation
atop a senseless heap of hurt and pain
There, she lay anguished and tormented: feeling
degraded, despised, devalued, defiled –
condemned to emotional decay

Thus she lay, totally curdled up: like a foetus!

Three long years later; and mid-way through the tale,
        the child's ordeal transformed into white-hot hell.
Masked and gagged; under thick cover of night,
        she was shipped off to a hard core sex house.
There, under lock–and–key; under-fed and under-nourished
she was forced into servicing a queue of Ten macho men.
Day-in and night-out; to endless eternity:
        she was paraded into hawking her fresh flesh,
        to fatten the rotten purse
        of her fortune-thirsty mistress!

To end the misery of her slavery, she went suicidal:
Her wretched body she hurled upon a speeding train.
Still conscious, she was promptly bundled off
        to a more secure predator's den:
From horrible hell, she arrived at the very gates of
        hideous Hades!
Chained, animal-like, her new master; unleashed himself
        upon her-
        brutally, cruelly, methodically: to sedate
        the sardonic fire burning in his loins.
Then, he loosed her into the lewd traffic of the open streets:
        to solicit the thirsty men of the midnight lust
        to quench the conflagration of their nightly rut.

Ultimately, the master moulded his young slave
        into a money-making machine: hawking
                intimate feminine flesh

in the dark of the seamy streets of the red district
of town
The monster of a master, turned his toilet into an
operations parlour –
A vile Palace for live shows of sensual
pornography,
A sensuous Studio of wicked abomination: in
which the child star
serviced the amorous libido of dogs!
Worse still, the ogre of a monster,
crudely castrated the womb of his baby protégé
to curtail accidental pregnancies from interrupting
the flood of revenues oozing from his money-
minting machine!
With this chilling surgery, the child died:
Her soul, she surrendered:
buried in the ghost of a zombie-like robot.

In due course, even the robot and the zombie
could absorb no more:
Arming itself with a strong stout golf club,
the zombie unleashed a barrage of blistering blows
to batter into a pulp, the skull of it's
monstrous master.
The implications of this near-homicide
touched the conscience of humanity's best-side.
In solidarity and fidelity to the cause,
women of courage sprang as one into action.
They reached out from the bounty of their compassion-
Stretched out their graceful hand of affection

to rescue the child from the ghastly pit of affliction:
To restore the dead, back to the living:
To reclaim the curled-up creature from its
Foetal Position!

02 March 2010, Maseru Sun Hotel, Room 426,
Maseru, Lesotho

DEDICATED to Abidemi Sanusi for her gripping
novel: 'EYO' on the occasion of its official launch in
Kenya and Uganda on 9th and 11th April, 2010 – by
the Publisher: WordAlive of Nairobi, Kenya.

The Young Warrior

Opio Dokotum Okaka

The young warrior
Heard the rev of the engine
And turned to have a look
He fingered the strap of his AK47
Assessing us in a moment of time
And with a broad smile
And open teeth
He lifted high a thick hand
And waved heartily
Before feeling his gun again,
Then he stroked one of his *emong* bulls
And tracked us with the side of his eye.

Welcome to my world!
Alakara adolun nakiyar kang!
He seemed to say,
You have not met me in a rage
After we have had an abortive raid,
You have not found me very wroth
After they have raided my father's *awii*,
For then I would be dangerous
To folks on my way; friend and foe.

You can wear all the suits in the world
As long as the cows are mine,
You can drive all those huge cars
So long as the cattle are mine,

You can heap certificates to the roof;
Know all the *ngaatuk* in the world are mine.

I saw him enter the thorny bushes
As we gratefully entered Moroto Town
Just as the sun after a long day's journey
Sunk into its resplendent bed in Lango.

Follow Me

Opio Dokotum Okaka

Follow me to the waves,
Let the current of my love
Flow through you
Like electricity from Owen Falls.

Follow me to the rivers,
Let the rising tide of my love
Sweep you into my arms
Like a gleeful baby lifted by a mother.

Follow me to the caves,
Let me show you my heart
Which I kept for you inside a pot
Securely hidden like Jeremiah's manna.

Follow me to the mountains,
Let me show you the kingdoms of my love
That I am going to give to you
To reign over all, as Queen of my heart.

Follow me to the clouds,
Let me teach you how to float
In the endless sky of my love,
Like a dry season eagle over our Lango sky.

Follow me around the cosmos,
Let me show you the height and the depth

The length and the width
The volume and density of this God-planted love.

Follow me to the many textures of my love,
Let me move your fingers on it like a carpenter's plane,
Feel it smooth and soft like a cat's fur
Or rough and hard like a rock hiding a precious mineral.

Follow me right to my father's house,
Turn the key and open my heart,
Fill all the rooms with the fullness of you,
Replace the blown bulbs with the light of your smiles,
For I am a pleasant surprise for you, from heaven:
Follow me; I say, follow me.

(28th April 2001)

Fifteen thousand dollars

Jennifer A. Okech

Fifteen thousand dollars!
He buried fifteen thousand dollars
The grim face weighed, and smiled
 At the one fifty new US dollar notes—
One, by one

The verdict was done;
My little tongue first,
My tear glands drained out
I'm resigned to my fate
I'm but an ordinary little soul—
Ordered by fate
To quench the thirst of an ignorant mind

Fifteen thousand dollars
Carried me into this darkness
Thirty, sore, scraggy treads
Beneath the magnificent gigantic beauty

Fifteen thousand dollars;
My heart, my liver—
My genitals,
Fifteen thousand dollars
Summed up my precious soul

The sorcerer mocks him;
Educated, but gullible!

Fifteen thousand dollars
Is how he summed me up—
To have the work of
His evil hands anointed
The gods needed to smile
Fifteen thousand dollars,
I shall never rest.

To Okot P'Bitek

Okot Benge

You are the living dead
For on the stone of our minds
You left deep footprints
That the winds of time shall never erase
Nor the rain of criticism weather away;
And when the sun of sanity has set
With our hands hankering for truth
We shall in the dark feel your footmarks.

Now we the young
With our tiny feet
Into your oversized footprints shall step
And hope with time our feet shall grow
To punch indelible marks like yours
On the everlasting rock of poetry.

The Wreck of a Nation

Okot Benge

Independence Day
The morning was bright
Optimistic
Pulsing with promises.

Then the mist stole in
Unnoticed, like a thief
Blanketing the land
In hopelessness

Night suddenly fell
Leaving us groping
For a goal missed

Yet peering through the thick fog
We witnessed an ordeal:

Mother Nation lay groaning
In labour pain
Struggling fruitlessly
To push out baby Future
While hyenas waited
With watery mouths

Then Doctor IMF stepped in
To hasten the birth
Mercilessly thumping the grotesque belly
Inserting red hot pincers

Into the birth canal
And mother Nation screamed
Engulfed in a whirlwind of hot pain.

It was a stillbirth
A dead Future
And mother Nation abandoned
To bleed to death.

An Appeal to Nature

Okot Benge

O wind! blow, blow!
Blow me some fresh air
For I am suffocating
With Man's rottenness at heart.

O Sun! shine, shine!
Shine me some light
For I am painfully lost
In Man's darkness in thoughts.

O Rain! fall, fall!
Fall and soften the world
For I am crushed
By the world's hardness and inhumanity.

O moon! smile, smile!
Smile me some comfort
For I am bogged down
In this marsh of disillusionment.

O Stars! twinkle, twinkle!
Twinkle me some hope
For I have lost faith
In myself and my God.

If I Am to Die

Okot Benge

If I am to die, sweet mother
Do not wax lachrymose
Do not drown in the sea of bitterness
Rend not your heart in anguish
For in dying I would have rested

I am tired, tired of floating
In this slow moving river of life
Full of snakes and crocodiles.
I am tired, tired of cruising my head
Against boulders of misfortunes
That leave my soul bruised and maimed
I am tired, tired of gulping down
The bitter waters of stark reality
That choke me with pain of frustration.

So, if I am to die, sweet mother
Just pray for my groping soul
Not with a bleeding tearful heart
But with the calm of dawn
For in dying I would have been freed.

Oh! I am tired, tired of flying
Through clouds of meaningless existence
That leave me unfulfilled and hollow.
I am tired, tired of always striving
To reach and hold the distant stars

That always twinkle in defiant mockery.
I am tired, tired of hanging in mid-air
With no soil or roots to sustain me
Slowly withering away into nothingness.

So, if I am to die, sweet mother
Lay the wreath of tranquillity on my grave
Make me a headstone of everlasting peace
For seven feet in the stomach of earth
I will be smiling with bitter contentment.

Nature's Orchestra

Jane P'Bitek Langoya Okot

The branches of the trees nod in unison
As the trees hum softly in rhythm to the rattling leaves
The flags stand at attention
And wave with as much dignity as they can muster

Then the invisible conductor gives the command

The dust swirls into action and dances the 'Twist-y'
Round and up, round and down, side to side, side to side.
Pieces of rubbish strewn by the roadside
Cannot resist the dance
As they fly higher and higher in the gust of wind.

The trees groan and creak in accord
As they try the '*pakachini*' dance.
The clouds rapidly gather
Followed closely by their notorious siblings.

At the signal of the invisible conductor
Lightning shows itself off with flashes in the sky
Like the blinking lights on the Christmas tree.
A prelude to the mighty drummer.
Like a classical music piece
The soft murmur of the drums rumbles to a crescendo
And climaxes to a thunderous roar!
Then drip and tap, drip and tap
Then larger drips and faster painful taps!

And finally the heavenly floodgates are opened
And the pounding rain joins in the chorus.
The parched earth opens up to greedily soak in the music
From nature's harmonious orchestra.

The invisible conductor gives the final command
And the music comes to a slow serene stop.

Man of God

Jane P'Bitek Langoya Okot

The fiery Pastor lifts high his Bible
In praise of the living God
Sprinkles of saliva shower his congregation
As he enthusiastically leads in worship
Pacing the length and breadth of the make-shift stage.

The way he shouts at God from time to time
One would be forgiven for imagining
That God is deaf.

He preaches hell-fire and damnation

'Happy are the poor' he shouts
'For they shall find riches in heaven!'
And the congregation gives its all in anticipation.

The man of God enriches himself on earth.
The monstrous fuel-guzzling machine
Is shamelessly parked besides the papyrus reed church.
And he lives in scandalous palaces and mansions
While the flock that he feeds off
Are up to their knees in squalour.

He shouts to the congregation to forgive others
So that God may forgive their trespasses
But his vengeance and revenge
On those who trespass against him
Are of ungodly proportions.

He does not practice what he preaches.
God must be nauseated
As he looks down at this imposter.

Sin Titulo 91

Julianne P'Bitek Okot

with hands on my shoulders
the man leads me
down a long hallway

past the rooms where women come undone
past christmas
& used wedding gowns for sale
past rooms with old laughter
sweating up the walls

he leads me
all the way down to Eve
who sits nude
& declares
that mercy is for losers
& condemns me
to liberation wars of convenience.

Sin Titulo 92

the man sits me
into a wooden chair

he removes the blindfold
what games are these, i ask

chance, liberation, war & mercy
you're now mine, he said

you're now mine
along with spike milligan & the goons
along with tattered manuals
old love poetry
you're now mine
i found you a spot on the shelf, see?

Sin Titulo 93

another man
a masked man
demands all
one hundred & sixty five kisses
if i have any expectation of release
so i tell him what i know to be true:

a lipsticked mouth must never be kissed
a lipsticked mouth is not for kissing
a lipsticked mouth is art
is protection
is political statement
is the distance between now & never

Sin Titulo 94

I'll love you in a minute, he says
blue on brown, blue on brown
I'll love you in a minute, he says
& in that chasm
nature unleashes itself
-- lightning strikes countless times

earthquakes, firestorms
children die & are born
die & are born again

in the minute I am waiting
terror smiles
blue on brown, blue on brown
as I wait for the world to settle

Sin Titulo 95

& then there were three men left in the country.
Actually, strictly speaking
there were two & a boy
but we call all of them men

the boy to remind us how to have sons
which is to say
that having sons is not like having daughters

the other is
pure & unadulterated pleasure
to remind us how to have a man
to say that having a woman
is not the same as having a man

the third is a man of the old kind
to remind us
that we need a man to tell us what to do
to remind us, we remind him
it feels necessary

because he has no other use
because we do what we need to do
whether or not he's there.

My Friend

Simon Peter Okwir

I cannot let you leave
I cannot let you perish
When I am able to help
I cannot let you
Suffer in the present
Because I know
The seal of our relationship is in our hearts.

I can bear the pain of your sorrow
More than you can ever know
I entreat you
Because you are a friend whom
I have laughed with
A friend whom I have cried with.

My friend, what would be the meaning of life
If the one with whom I share a ripe fruit is not with me?
What would be the meaning of life
If the one with whom we eat words of life is not with me?

My friend
Indeed to have known
A friend like you
Is the best gift
Life could ever give me.

Atyeno

James Onono

This is the season
The white ants will soon be leaving the anthill
The edible ants will soon fly the Gulu sky
Heavy sleepers will miss Atyeno
For Atyeno comes out late in the night

The Great Northern Doctor

James Onono

Among heroes,
The great Northern Doctor
Who, like Emmanuel,
Died for the flock

Lukwiya worked with truth and dignity
But in the line of duty, he perished
The fallen Pillar of Lacor, his shoes lie abandoned,
For none has dared wear them

Among the Heroes of Uganda,
Among the honored,
There is no greater sacrifice than that of a life
Rest in Peace, son of Matayo

Although Ebola, snatched you
Never will you be forgotten
On their way to collect firewood, women sing your name
On their way to the well, they still sing your name.

All I have

Jackson Dre Otim

Tamara, if you have to go,
Please do not go with my heart
It's all I have when you are gone.

For My Mother

Moses Agaba Rubalema

In her, I had a home for nine months.
She felt bags of pain giving me life
But she still held me up in her hands and said,
"I love you my baby boy."

Like a parasite I fed on her,
I soiled her.
I cried her out of sleep
But she bathed me and put me back to sleep

She did not just watch me.
She propped me up to sit.
Clapped for me to stand up.
She beckoned me to crawl
Walked me through my walking troubles.
When I fell she held me and said that was great!

She taught me to eat
She became my baby and played with me
We danced and laughed together
She held my hand to school
Ate saltless food for my school fees.

But then
It did not matter
She was my mother after all.

And then
Just when I was beginning to realise her struggles
Just when I wanted us to speak adult to adult
My mother was gone
She was gone,
Gone to a place where I could not reach her.

All I had were bits and pieces
Of our moments together

Life History of the Tree

Isaac Settuba

The tree has gone barren
For seasons, hardly a fruit, a leaf
Nor a colouring flower;
But for long did you savour
And soundly did you nap.

The trunk and branches are dead dry
The feet planted in cracked ground;
But in such dryness some soils hold
And the trunk is wall to lean on
When backs are much worked.

Trunk and branches are rock hard
The bark peeling and prickly;
But much better for local government
To nail solemn announcement,
And blossoming boys may climb for fun
As good parents pluck off stick
To bounce off shorts and skirts
In stern correction.

Neither cut nor uproot
Let the greedy fires starve.

(Addis Ababa, November 2015)

Divide and Share

Issac Settuba

The kill is on my table
I am to reduce it to meat
To which you all have
Right to share.

And to come near this table;
Be of my blood-like or kin
With or without DNA,
Be my dear in-law
In legality or freedom,
Be my beloved spouse
In love or convenience,
Be of my ways
Sincere or interested.

But always blow the trumpet loud
The lungs full or empty,
And the choicest of pieces
Shall surely come your way.

(Addis Ababa, April 2014)

The Promised Land

Ernest Katwesigye Tashobya

We were in bondage to despotism,
But we ate to our fill;
We labored under the yoke of slavery of restless sleep,
But had a decent shelter.

Then you came: the Prophet,
With your promise of bliss:
"I will lead you to the promised land,
A land flowing with milk and honey."

We were apprehensive,
But you persuaded us God had sent you.
Your guerilla miracles wowed Pharaoh,
And he freed us into your liberation arms.

A potentially three days' journey,
Turned into a 30 years' trek and counting;
As we moved in circles,
Through the wilderness.

You fed us on manna of retrenchment,
Saying it was the cost of development;
You supplied us hard water of privatisation from the rock,
Promising a better tomorrow.

In the place of milk,
We feast on inflation;

Rather than mouth dripping honey,
We choke on corruption.

Fatigued, we still wait to reach the Promised Land,
Hanging on unfulfilled promises;
The prophet is aging fast,
And losing vision – of the Promised Land.

Verdict

Isaac Tibasiima

We eagerly await your baby
And with a smile
We welcome it.

We sit around the fire
Warming our chat and throats with drink
Thinking, turning, nodding heads
We jump up in excitement at the baby
Yet, some of us
Simply coil at its existence.

'Awful!' one of us exclaims
'Splendid,' retorts the other
'Nay,' a voice interrupts.
'There is a complexion out of place here'
'Argh, this is archaic, not our baby type'

We think of individual concepts
And the baby must prove them
We argue over what is not
And get lost in what is
We raise hands at each other
Point to a dark force rejecting our stand.
Our voices now raised
Put out the peaceful night it should be.

Our concept is dead
we are disappointed

Now
We will not see!
We refuse to accept the baby.
'But', one of us comes in
'It is a baby'
'Of course it is!' one screams
'But not my type of baby'.

A fight ensues
We agree on this
Reject this and the other idea
Shake our heads in anger.
We make the baby ours
And forget the hours of labour
We forget the gestation period
We only see the product
Now we look for what is not.

We make our judgement
And that shall stand
This baby shall face its fate
Each baby has gone through this pain:

For some, there is a life
Some actually live for a while
We massacre most
And kill them by our argument
For we hold them in the cold,
They say it is not good for their lungs:
They die.

We sit back
Happy at each let to live
But happier at each let to die
In the name of standard
In the name of authenticity
In the name of a birthright
In the name of... What shall I call it?
Criticism.

(For Beverley, Edwin and John)

Deathly Pale

Isaac Tibasiima

From above
The blue clouds
Hide the unseen canopy
Of what would be beautiful.

We descend
And all the time
The coldness grips me
And takes my breath away.

Did I foresee this?
Did I think of this?

The trees are asleep
The lakes hard solid
The land white

What happened to life
The beauty I once beheld?
What happened to grass
That could always be seen green?
Dead, silently dead.

The people go on
Shrouded like babies in shawls
Fear grips me,
Suddenly

And I am sure, very sure
This is worse.

I smoke, suddenly,
My African warmth swallowing the cold
And God, it too dies out.

I get out of it
Into a beautiful white
That only covers a pale countryside
A dead one to be sure.
My heart beats more
As I move to another world
One of uncertainty
For the next weeks.

I am nostalgic,
Oh, I miss the sun
I miss the tropical African sun

And here,
God help these fellows!

(Inspired by Heathrow, London)

The Bishop is Coming

Isaac Tibasiima

We shall straighten our paths
Make all the rooms clean
Because in them he shall peep
And sigh with gladness
'My children, you are clean'

We shall put on our best
Those rags and rubbish shall be hidden
We shall not be caught unawares
Because we should be commended
And thumbs shall definitely be up.

Oh, the Bishop is coming
O, so I thought, he is
I shall work my best
I shall be glued to my desk
And yes, he shall surely see the worker in me.

We raise our hands
And in ululation, welcome him
So he has come, so he has come
But, is....
Never mind, he is here.

And so he comes
He does not even get to the clean places
But rushes to see

Just the filth in us
Openly telling our hypocrisy from sight
For he looks at us intently

Deep within
We see the look of mockery
But then, who cares
We are glad he has come
And the grin on his face
Shows it all

He is definitely glad.

*(Written in anticipation of the Visit from The Bishop of
Lugazi to St Noa Mawaggali SS, Jinja, 2012)*

Who Extinguished the Fire

James Turyatemba

Who extinguished the fire in the homestead?
Did he consult the elders
Or was it recommended
By environmentalists?

Was it because the fog
Had receded to the valleys
As hills became warmer?
Was it because the smoke
Made our eyes water
And our noses run?

Was it a strategy
Of tactical retreat
To deny mosquitoes a
Sumptuous evening meal
As we imbibed the wise axioms
Of our greying elders?

Sound the drums
For the elders to converge!
Divulge the secret
That their cultural code
Has been adulterated!

The ashes have been cleared
And fortified prisons erected
The new curriculum is foreign
Irrelevant and obsolete!

Wake up Africa

James Turyatemba

Wake up Africa
My beloved continent
Is it conventional
To soundly snore
When you are wide awake?

Why snooze in noisy slums
With bullets ripping the air?
Does the quietness beyond
Make you nervous?

Are you pathetically insane
Or slightly demented
Why court poverty
By borrowing today
To pay yesterday's debts?

Are repressive wars
And wanton genocide
A form of family planning?
Should dictators overthrow dictators
To entrench systematic dictatorships?

Wake up Africa
You have slept long enough
Such a deep slumber
Is counter productive
In this prime millennium!

The Last Photograph

Jotham Tusingwire

He wondered whether what the mirror reflected was him:
The hollowed cheeks, protruding bones, pale face,
The falling off hair, the scaly complexion…

He couldn't explain his recent rapid weight loss,
Waning appetite, running stomach, constant
        headache…

Weren't these clear symptoms?
What else did he need to prove his fears?

At once he embarked on a journey into his past.
A string of all his girlfriends unravelled before him…
He critically scrutinised the long list
He endeavoured to figure out the most likely suspect:

He plunged into his suitcase and plucked out his album
And turned page by page, admiring, hating, suspecting
Reminiscing, regretting, longing…

Each of them seemed to have donated a dose of fate
Yet he could almost acquit all of them…

After three analytical, critical rounds at each,
He resolved that all were guilty.

He pulled out Irene's photo, held it from the edge
And set it alight
Then Carol, Cathy, Jane, Phyllis, Amanda…

The room was full of smoke and the smell of chemicals.

Then crisis came…He picked Nectar's photo.
He gazed into her laughter-filled eyes, at the full
luscious
          lips,
Graceful neck, dark, well-knit hair
The round buttocks that filled the white plastic chair
–
The legs that flowed onto the green carpet of grass…

The Aphrodite face that glowed under the shade
Of the purple bougainvillea in the Calypso gardens…
Then the chest that pushed the pink blouse
Like the nibs of ball-point pens…

An inevitable grin registered on his lips…
Nectar's laughter resounded in his ears
He could smell the fragrance of her "Innocence"
perfume
Feel the touch of her silky hands
And O…those warm romantic nights…

He felt his lachrymals release warm tears
He let them flow freely down his cheeks...

Then, he suddenly shouted: No! Never!
I will never burn you, sweet Nectar
Not if you were to kill me a million times!

He rushed into his bed, clasped Nectar's photo by his heart
Blanketed himself, and was soon on tour in
slumberland.

The man in the mirror

Henry 'THB' Twahirwa

Last night I stood in front of a mirror
But the strange man;
That strange man in front of me,
Didn't seem happy to see me.

He acted like he knew me from somewhere
Like he had a bone to pick with me.
But I was certain that we had never crossed paths.
Besides, he looked like those crazy types
So, he was obviously from different circles.
Not my circles, definitely not;
We don't hang out with people like him.

He didn't even have the common courtesy
To give me a pretentious handshake.
Not even a verbal greeting!
He just squinted and nodded in my direction.
What a pathetic lack of culture!

But it's his peculiar aloofness
That unlocked my curiosity.
And in a split of a second,
Much to my surprise,
I was standing next to him;
Trying to see past his now, poker face.
But I couldn't get far;
I couldn't figure this strange man out!

Freedom

Henry 'THB' Twahirwa

Freedom is a lot like a beautiful maiden
Seated at the other end of the dance floor.
If you desire to take your chance on a dance with her
You've got to be both gentle and aggressive.
You've got to give off that bitter-sweet charm
To make her raise into your arms
And melt in them.

Don't just sit back and daydream,
About what you two could do to each other;
It never pays off.
For she might wind up in the arms of another
Who is faster on his feet.
You've got to spring onto your feet
With a famished tiger's vigour
And walk over to her,
With a cat's poise.
And before you know it,
You will swing her to your rhythm,
And she will be yours.

Silence

Hilda Twongyeirwe

silence fills our mouths
not in Judge Joan Kagezi's death
but in the eerie shadows that lark in the dark
these days of 30th March 2015.
Silence grips our hearth
not in the Xenophobia bodies on display on pavements
but hearts warming
to the smell of burning blood
in Johannesburg.

this silence
gropes us
fills us
with a hollowness.

Greet Africa when you return

Hilda Twongyeirwe

I greet you Africa
I greet you from Cape to Cairo
I hug you with arms of my sister from Somalia
She implored me;
       Greet Africa when you return.

At Southern Theatre we met
On a gray Scandinavian evening
But the African sun still shone in her eyes
The effusive Nile flowed into our handshake
Connecting us in an embrace
Of what we share
Of what we are.

But I felt a fear tear into her voice
It wrapped her tongue when she spoke
       This place my sister
       Sucks something out of you
       So you are not you
       You are you
       But you are not you
       Just greet Africa when you return.

I greet you Africa
I greet you with her sacrifice of tears
I dare cleanse you of bloodstains that have denied
          her home
She implored me;

Tell Africa
Her children abroad are roadside stones.

(Sept 2010)

At Leo Tolstoy's Graveside

Hilda Twongyeirwe

Unperturbed,
weeds grow,
wild, like Anna Karenin spirit,
rubbing palms, kissing, whispering, swaying,
on the small rectangle in the woods
unaware of Leo Tolstoy
who lives
beneath
in pursuit of quiet and solitude.

(03/09/2014)

V-Power

Hilda Twongyeirwe

We need a new name
simple, like Nosebleed
one we can quickly say
without stopping to check.

We need a definitive name
not visitors are in town
moon colour has changed
the city here is invaded.

We need a new name
a name which will freely
glide
through
lips.

Poetic Quintet

Timothy Wangusa

Wakhutu ni Nase
(Natsya, Natsya, Natsya)

Natsya, natsya, natsya
Natuy'e 'khutu 'yo
Ni babaana bewe
Isya busima!

Yalom'eri, 'Syeelekho.

Nasya, nasya, nasya
Nanosya nga siina!

Yalom'eri, Fuk'e 'ndye
Na--fuka, na--fuka, na--fuka
Nayiisa nga siina!

Yalom'e 'ri, Fuumul'e 'ndye.

O-o, ka kukhutu 'ku!
O-o, kuri bibyange busa!
Kuri byo'mukooko wase!

Nase nakuloma ndi –
Tsy'o 'kkholele 'taayi!
Naanu utamba siina?
Naanu 'khali nu mukooko?
Bon'o 'milyokhosa bilyo!
Bon'o 'khobolaka tsinyenyi!

ortoise and I
(I Went, Went, Went)

I went, went, went
Till I came across a tortoise
With its children
Grinding millet!

Help me to grind, it said.

I ground, ground, ground
Till the flour was so fine!

Cook for me to eat, it said.
mingle-mingle-cooked
The meal was so well done!

Serve me to eat, it said.

My, what a tortoise this is!
My, says it is all his!
Says it all belongs to his sister!

So I told him off and said –
Stop your loud nonsense!
Who has nothing of his own?
Who is without a sister?
See how you munch with greed!
See how you gobble the sauce!

O-o, ka kukhutu'ku!   My, what a tortoise this is!
O-o, kuri bibyange busa!   My, it says it is all his!
Kuri byo'mukooko wase!   Says it all belongs to his sister!

Tsh! Yisyenda nase nikhale!   Tsh! You move over, so I also sit!
Tsh! Lekhelaawo nase 'ndye!   Tsh! You stop there, so I also eat!

Kumwenya Kwe Khusya Bulo (Kumuunyu kwe Mbeba)

Song of the Millet Grinders (The Soup of a Rat)

Kumuunyu kwe mbeba   O the soup of a rat,
    Kufuura kwe nyama!   Beats the soup of beef!
Kumuunyu kwe mbeba   O the soup of a rat
    Kufuura kwe ngokho!   Beats the soup of chicken!
       ***   ***

Khusundesunde kumukhebo   Let's quick-grind the millet
Khusundesunde kumukhebo   Let's quick-grind the millet

Kwa Mayi Nelima   Of our mother Digging-month[1]
Kwa Mayi Nalyaaka   Of our mother Weeding-month[2]
Kwa Mayi Namunaane   Of our mother Rainiest-month[3]
Kwa Mayi Nekesa   Of our mother Harvest-month[4]

Isyo khu lusisi   Baby grinding-stone on mother-stone
Isyo khu lusisi   Baby grinding-stone on mother-stone

Lutsyo khu mayika   Mingling-pot onto firestones
Lutsyo khu mayika   Mingling-pot onto firestones

Kumukango mu lutsyo   Mingling-stick into mingling-pot
Kumukango mu lutsyo   Mingling-stick into mingling-pot

| Busima khu lweelo | Millet meal onto wooden platter |
| Busima khu lweelo | Millet meal onto wooden platter |

Kamakhaayi mu ndubi	End-scraps from pot into basket
Kamakhaayi mu ndubi	End-scraps from pot into basket
Tsinyenyi mu sibuumba	The sauce into clay bowl
Tsinyenyi mu sibuumba	The sauce into clay bowl

Khulye bukalalaasi	And we eat the grinders' feast
Khulye bukalalaasi	And we eat the grinders' feast
Ni kumuunyu kwe mbeba	O with the soup of a rat
Kufuura kwe nyama!	That beats the soup of beef!
Ni kumuunyu kwe mbeba	O with the soup of a rat
Kufuura kwe ngokho!	That beats the soup of chicken!

***

Buufu bupaakhibwe	Let the flour be soaked with water
Babupaakhe bururutse	Let it ferment to the full
Khumala biffukhu musaafu	For seven days long
Lwanyuma babukhalaange	Then on an open fire let it be baked
Namwe ta babufuluke	Or else be boiled into soft porridge.

| Khulye khu muuma | Let's eat of the baked noodles |
| Khukhombe ni khu buyu; | Let's taste the fermented porridge; |

Kametsi mu muuma	And now water into the noodles
Limela mu nyungu;	Millet yeast added to the clay pot
Nio tsimuuma tsirokore	To let the noodles gurgle
Ni buyu bubiitake!	And the fermented porridge bubble!

| Khawiiwi khu sipaanga | Brew-prone insects upon the clay pot |
| Khasabamalwa mu sawu | Brew-beggar's herb hidden in his pocket |

Sisawuli khu lusekhe	Mini sieve at bottom end of drinker's tube
Lusekhe mu maange –	Drinkers' tubes into giant clay pot –
Khunywe khwinukune	To drink we do with utter relish
Khunywe khusangaale	We drink and jubilate thereby
Khunywe khusakalale	We drink and swell inwardly
Khunywe khukangulukhe –	We drink and become unbound –
Khusindule kamabeka	And we execute the dances
Khukhine luhengele	We dance the inverted wooden tray
Khukhine lituungu	We dance the seven-string *litungu*
Khukhine sitingiti	We dance the two-string *sitingiti*
Khupe bikalakala	As we utter sharp ululations
Ni bikalakasya	Mixed with sounds of highest pitch
Ni bikhonyakisya	And sounds of things knocking about
Ni bikulungusya…	And sounds of things rolling around…

***

Kumuunyu kwe mbeba	O the soup of a rat
Kufuura kwe nyama	Beats the soup of beef!
Kumuunyu kwe mbeba	O the soup of a rat
Kufuura kwe ngokho	Beats the soup of chicken!

***

Sunda, sunda, khangu!	Grind, grind, quick!
Sunda kumukhebo!	Grind, grind the millet
Isyo khu lusisi	Baby grinding-stone on mother-stone
Lutsyo khu mayika –	Mingling-pot onto firestones –

Sunda, sunda, sunda!	Grind, grind, grind!
Bakhaana, sunda, sunda	Girls, grind, grind
Bakhaana, sunda, sunda –	Girls, grind, grind –
Bakhana, sundasunda	
kumukhebo!	Girls, quick-grind the millet!

The A-Z of the Perpetual Father

(For Fathers Union Day, Mbale Diocese, 2006)

Timothy Wangusa

Between faithfully husbanding his only wife
And generating the couple's precious replicas,
The exemplary perpetual father should manifest
The **A-Z** paternal attributes as named hereunder:

A= Accommodating all antics and accidents
B= Bearing with the bride upon every bump
C= Cherishing the children from their childhood
D= Defending any domesticated dos and don'ts
E= Exhibiting excellence by example
F= Fairness in fending for the family
G= Grooming them to go on growing
H= Hating to have the home humiliated
I= Immunity to insinuations of the in-laws
J= Justice in judging the juniors
K= Kindling kindness in the kids
L= Loving the lazy and the lukewarm
M= Merciful in meting out any measures
N= Neither niggardly nor negligent
O= Open-handed to offspring and orphans
P= Praying and playing as part of the plan
Q= Quick to quit a quarrel
R= Repaying recklessness with rectitude
S= Steadfast from Sabbath to Sabbath
T= Trained to tame the tongue
U= Uniquely unequivocal and unwavering

V= Vulnerable but virtuous and victorious
W= Wondrous waiter upon the weak
X= X-phobic about x-marrieds and x-lovers
Y= Yearly yielding to the yoke
Z= Zealously zooming or zigzagging to Zion.

Intelligent Design

Timothy Wangusa

Hullo you there, Intelligent Design!

For I hear that is the ultra-scientific name,
Fabricated in USA
In the Year of Development 1989,
For whatever you might be –

To signify the expulsion of God
From the nation's classrooms,
Thereby insulating the sprouting soul
From all culture-centred biases…

Are you, nonetheless –
He
She
It
He-she
She-he or
He-it-she?

Do you have –
Eyes
Ears
Nose
Mouth
Teeth
Tongue
Limbs

Finger-nails
Toe-nails
Bones
Skeleton
Muscle
Marrow
Blood
Plasma
Lymph
Skin
Hair
Brain
Intestines
Lungs
Spleen
Kidneys
Bladder
Bowels
Guts
Prostate
Ovaries
Genitals and
Gender?

Do you comprise –
Atoms
Neurons
Nucleuses
Molecules
Chromosomes

Particles
Fragments
Genes and
Bindings?

Or are you –
Impulses
Pulsations
Sensations
Passion
Compassion
Spark
Fire
Flame
Spectre
Spectrum
Shade
Shadow
Silhouette or
Spirit?

Do you have –
Shape
Form
Mass
Volume
Content
Context
Origin
Identity

Source
Cause
Course
Direction
Locus
Choice
Purpose
Voice
Words
Speech
Meaning
Goal
Destiny and
Destination?

Might you be –
Prior
Pre-existent
Post-existent
Concurrent
Contemporaneous
Instant
Constant
Space-less
Ultra-wave
Ethereal
Virtual
Digital
Cyclical
Spherical

Multi-geometric
Multi-dimensional
Tangential
Trans-linear
Trans-numeric
Trans-sensory
Retro-chronometric
Post-chronometric and
Trans-chronological?

Could you be –
Phenomenon prior to conception,
Reality beyond perception,
Despair of definition,
Discovery of the destitute,

Or otherwise –

What are you?
And what are you not?

THE EVOLUTIONARY BIBLE

THE FIRST BOOK OF MOSES, CALLED GENESIS

Timothy Wangusa

1 Approximately 13.8 billion years ago (that is, backwards from 2016 AD), God spoke the universe into instant being with a big bang!

2 Prior to that point there was no space, no duration, that is, no sky and atmosphere and no time lapse – all pre-creation living entities that there were did exist without need of celestial expanse.

3 These were God himself, the upright angels, and the fallen angels.

4 The universe that God had thus caused to happen comprised of numberless stars, both the visible and the invisible, fixed in immense space that has no boundaries and no end; that is to say, it is infinite.

5 There is an observable universe; and there is an unobservable universe, which is un-measurable and un-comprehensible.

6 The observable universe consists of hundreds of billions (more than 10^{11}) galaxies;

7 And each galaxy (or constellation) consists of stars (or suns) that range from _dwarfs_ with just a few *thousand* (10^3) stars to *giants* with one hundred _trillion_ (10^{14}) stars, each orbiting their galaxy's own _centre of mass_.

8 And God saw that everything that He had made and set in motion for the next 8,232,000,000 years was good; and He called all that creation phase, One Day.

9   And, on the heavenly calendar, there was evening, and there was morning – *the first cosmic day.*

10 Next, some 4,568,000,000 (that is, 4.6 billion) years ago, God commanded the Solar System to occur within the womb of the universe;

11 And this came to pass as a result of the gravitational collapse of a giant molecular cloud, which gave rise to the Sun together with its orbiting group of the as yet known eight planets as well as the smaller objects such as dwarf planets and small Solar System bodies, examples of which are comets and asteroids.

12 The Solar System is only one grouping among 220 billion stars that constitute our particular galaxy, the Milky Way.

13 The distances between the stars are so mind-boggling that they are best expressed in terms of light-years –

14 A light-year being the distance that light travels in one solar year; that is, 186, 000 (miles per second) x 60 x 60 x 24 x 365.25 = approx 5,869,713,600,000 miles = approx 9,391,541,760,000 kilometres .

15 The nearest star to the Solar Sun – the star Proxima Centauri – is 4.22 light-years away, which is approx 39,632,306,227,200 kilometres.

16 The Solar System is located 26,000 light-years from the centre of the Milky Way;

17 While the Milky Way is about 100,000 light-years across; and at its centre (as is the case with the centre of most galaxies) there is a monstrous black hole, billions of times as massive as the sun -

18 A black hole being a massive void or abyss comprising an original volume of space-time, that came into being at the genesis of the universe, which has a gravitational field so intense that its escape velocity equals or exceeds that of light;

19 But in a percentage of the monstrously extensive black holes, the black hole is caused by a star in the last phase of its evolution, in which the star collapses, creating a similar gravitational field.

20 The Milky Way does not sit still, but is constantly rotating through space – at the same time as it moves outwards within the womb of an ever-expanding visible universe.

21 All the stars in the visible universe are forever in motion, whizzing away at the average speed of 792,000 kilometres per hour, or 220 kilometres (= *Kampala to Kumi*) per second.

22 The Solar System in particular travels at an average speed of 515,000 miles per hour (828,000 kilometres per hour = 229 kilometres per second). Even at this very rapid speed, the Solar System would take about 230 million years to travel all the way around the Milky Way.

23 And God saw that everything that He had done in causing the Solar System to happen was good; and all the duration from the emergence of the planets through billions of years of their mellowing to a decimal point of their original temperatures, He called it One Day.

24 And, on the heavenly calendar, there was evening, and there was morning – *the second cosmic day.*

2 A thousand years in God's sight are like one evening gone by; yesterday today and tomorrow all exist simultaneously before Him – *and He can today cause something tomorrow to alter something yesterday!*

2 Creating something instantly is as good to Him as moulding it over one billion years; and that is the case with life on the unique planet Earth.

3 Of all the planets of the Solar System, He equipped Earth with the appropriate geology and atmosphere (of air and water) for originating and sustaining biological existence.

4 **(To be continued...)**

Life is a Gift

Subira Yamumpa

Life is a gift to be grateful for
Before you think of saying unkind words
Think of someone who cannot speak
Before you say you are stressed
Think of someone on his deathbed.

Before you complain about your children
Think of someone who is barren
Before you complain about your nagging partner
Think of someone crying out to God for a
companion.

Before you complain about your job
Think of millions unemployed
Before you complain about the taste of your food
Think of multitudes with nothing to eat.

Before you complain about the distance you drive
Think of someone who walks the same distance
Before you disobey your parents
Think of millions of orphans.

Before you complain about your small house
Think of babies living on the streets
Before you complain at all
Remember you are alive.

Notes on Contributors

Susan Nalugwa Kiguli is an academic and poet. She holds a PhD in English from The University of Leeds (UK) sponsored by the Commonwealth Scholarship Scheme. She was the African Studies Association Presidential Fellow, 2011 and this presented her with an opportunity to read her poetry at the Library of Congress, Washington DC in November, 2011. She has served as the chairperson of FEMRITE, Uganda Women Writers' Association. She currently serves on the Advisory Board for the African Writers Trust (AWT). She was the chief convener for Celebrating Ugandan Writing: Okot p'Bitek's Song of Lawino at 50 held at Makerere University in March, 2016. She is the author of The African Saga and Home Floats in a Distance/Zuhause Treibt in der Ferne(Gedichte): a bilingual edition in English and German. Prossy Abalo is a high school student and a member of FEMRITE Creative Writing club in Gulu Army Secondary School.

Mwalimu Austin Bukenya is a Ugandan poet, playwright, novelist and academic. He is the author of the novel; The People's Bachelor, and a play; The Bride. He has taught languages, literature and drama at Makerere University in Uganda and universities in the UK, Tanzania and Kenya since the late 1960s. He has also held residences at universities in Rwanda and Germany. Bukenya is also a literary critic, novelist, poet and dramatist. An accomplished stage and screen actor, he was, for several , years Director of the Creative and Performing Arts Centre at Kenyatta University, in Nairobi, Kenya.

Richard Aboko is a high school teacher of Literature and English at St Henry's College Kitovu, Masaka.

Pamela Acaye Elizabeth is an actress, fitness instructor, designer, producer and director of theater productions in Uganda and greater East Africa. Vogue Italia magazine, in June 2012 featured her as one of the Social activists Africa should look out for.

Vicky Achiro is a member of FEMRITE Creative Writing club in Alliance High School, Gulu.

Gloria Adoch is a member of FEMRITE Creative Writing club in Sacred Heart Secondary School in Gulu, also recipient of Tukosawa Creative writing Award 2015

Earnest Ainembabazi hails from Isingiro in western Uganda. He holds a Master of Arts degree from Kyambogo University. He is a High School teacher of English language and literature.

Lillian Akampurira Aujo is a lawyer by profession, winner of the inaugural BNP Award and a member of FEMRITE.

Melvin Vincent Akankwasa is a recipient of the 2008 National Book Trust of Uganda Literary Award in Short Story Writing Competitions - Primary School Level. That was while he was a pupil at Buganda Road Primary school. He was a volunteer at the Tukosawa Stars Creative Writing Workshop in Gulu in 2015.

Charlotte Akello is student of Biomedical Sciences at Makerere University. She started writing seriously at the age of 17. She is passionate about poetry.

Brenda Rachel Alaroker is a member of FEMRITE Creative Writing club in Sacred Heart Secondary School, Gulu.

Ivan Aloya is a member of FEMRITE Creative Writing club in Gulu Army Secondary School.

Harriet Anena is a poet and writer from Gulu. She is the author of *A Nation In Labour* – a collection of social conscience poetry. Her poems and short stories have also been published on other platforms in and outside Uganda. In 2013, she was shortlisted for the Ghana Poetry Prize.

Bruce Arinaitwe is a member of FEMRITE Creative Writing club in Kigezi High School, Kabale.

Bonnetvanture Asiimwe is a visual artist and poet.

Jackie Asiimwe is a lawyer by Profession, a poet, a feminist, and a passionate human rights activist.

Regina Asinde is a freelance editor, poet and writer who finds freedom in words. In 2010, she was the 2nd winner in the BNPA poetry Award. Her poems have been published in the anthologies and online magazines.

Sophie Bamwoyeraki was head of the English and Literature Dept at Kampala International School. She has co-authored English Course books for secondary and Primary schools. Her poems feature in a number of anthologies in Uganda and South Africa. Her debut poetry collection co-authored with Jane Okot **P'Bitek Langoya was released in 2016.**

Violet Barungi's Play; Over my Dead Body, won the British Council New Playwriting Award for Africa in 1997. She is the author of acclaimed novels; The Shadow and the Substance (1998) and Cassandra 1999.

Bwambale Mugati is a High school Teacher of Literature and English Language. He teachers at Sir Samuel Baker Secondary school, Gulu.

Richard Chole is a High School Teacher of literature and English language currently stationed at PMM Girls' School in Jinja. He is keen to provide opportunities for teenagers to explore their creative writing abilities.

Janny Ekyasiimire is a member of FEMRITE Creative Writing club in Kigezi High School, Kabale.

David Patrick Emiru is a writer who up-till about now, keeps most of his writings to himself and to very small audiences for purposes feedback.

Laban Erapu is a Professor of Literature and a published poet and writer. He is a Senior lecturer at Bishop Stuart University, Mbarara.

Samuel Iga Zinunula is an Agriculturalist by profession, a businessman by occupation and a poet by vocation.

Peter Kagayi Mutanga is a published and performance poet. He is a graduate of law from Makerere University. His debut poetry collection; The Headline that Morning, came out in 2016.

Danson. S. Kahyana is a published author and a lecturer in the Department of Literature, Makerere University.

Betty Kaigo is a member of FEMRITE and a High School teacher of literature and English Language.

Samuel Kamugisha is a Ugandan journalist and fiction writer. In 2015, he won the Monitor Publications Tebere - Mudini Award, for his academic excellence. He is an editor with The Tower Post (www.thetowerpost.com) and HotSpot Ug (www.hotspot.ug).

Hope Kansiime is a poet and a graduate of Mass communication from Makerere University.

Jacob Katumusiime, former President of the MUK Literature Association (LITASS) is obsessed with word-craft. He likes writing poetry and teaching African Literature. He performs his poetry at many different platforms.

Aloysius Kawooya is a member of the FEMRITE Readers/ Writers Club.

Gloria Kiconco is a correspondent for Commonwealth Writers. Her personal essays have appeared in the The Forager Magazine and Doppiozero's Why Africa? Her poetry has been published in Brittle Paper, Lawino, So Many Stories and on her blog, otherandelse.wordpress.com.

MildredBarya Kiconco 's first book of poetry, Men Love Chocolate But They Don't Say (2002), won the National Poetry Award in Uganda. Her second and third collections; The Price of Memory After The Tsunami and Give me Room to Move my Feet, were published later to much critical acclaim. She has also published short stories.

Melissa Kiguwa is an artist, a daughter, and a radical feminist. Raised by a Haitian father and a Ugandan mother, Melissa Kiguwa considers herself an afro-nomad. Her work focuses on imperialism, migration, sexuality, spirituality, and trauma. In her works she re-imagines liberation, new horizons, and afro legacy-building.

Bob Kisiki is a novelist, poet, playwright and newspaper columnist with New Vision. He has published three novels; *The Kind Gang, Gobah & the Killer Healers* and *The Rainbow's End* and a children's storybook; Kibediko. He is a manager with Rhema Books Ltd, a publishing firm.

Brian Kenneth Kissa is passionate about creative writing. He is a Ugandan and is currently pursuing a Bachelor of Arts degree in English language and literature Education at Makerere university.

Betty Kituyi is a published poet and a writer. She is a member of FEMRITE.

George Kiwanuka loves writing and reading widely and fears that if the young generation is not taught to carry on the culture of writing, future generations will have nothing preserved for them to read.

Juliet Kushaba is a published writer of short stories and essays.

Alice Tumwesigye Kyobutungi is a Senior Lecturer at Bishop Stuart University, Mbarara. She is a published poet and author of other academic works.

Mercy Aweko Nimungu is a member of FEMRITE Creative Writing club in Gulu High School.

Sonia Koheirwe is a member of FEMRITE Creative Writing club in Kigezi High School, Kabale.

Steven Lubangakene is a member of FEMRITE Creative Writing club in Gulu Army Secondary School.

Susan Malinga is a Human Resource Consultant, Management Trainer, Counselor, Mentor and Coach. She has a Bachelors degree in Social Sciences (Hons) from Makerere University and a Masters degree in Human Resource Management from Uganda Management Institute (UMI). She is also a passionate poet.

Solomon Manzi is a member of the Lantern Meet of Poets, Uganda.

Mbabazi Kahirwa lives in Uganda with a mother that loves him dearly. He attends law school and is a lover of all things beautiful.

Praise Mugisha is a member of FEMRITE Creative Writing club in Kigezi High School, Kabale.

Bernard Mujuni who works with Ministry of Gender Labour and Social Development has been a closet poet. This is his maiden publication.

Edna Namara is a teacher of English Language and Literature. She is a member of FEMRITE.

Beverley Nambozo Nsengiyunva is a Poet, Writer, Children's Enthusiast, Founder of Babishai Niwe Poetry Foundation.

Rashida Namulondo is a Performance poet, a youth worker and an actress. She is a lover of storytelling and uses the gift in her mentorship work in schools.

Agness Namusisi is a member of FEMRITE Creative Writing Club in Alliance High School, Gulu.

Jason Sabiiti Ntaro is a performance poet. He hails from a district of hard energetic workers; Kabale, at the shores of Africa's deepest Lake, Bunyonyi. His first appearance on the public stage was in 2007, with Lantern Meet of Poets. Since then, Ntaro has performed at multiple poetry platforms in East Africa.

Joel Benjamin Ntwatwa loves art and its aesthetics. He won three National Book Trust of Uganda Awards (NABOTU) at national level in 1999, 2000 and 2001 for his poetry.

Calvin Ocitti is a member of FEMRITE Creative Writing Club in Samuel Baker Secondary School, Gulu.

Julius Ocwinyo is a published novelist. One of his novels; Fate of the Banished, is taught as a set book on the Secondary Curriculum.

Lawrance Max Odongo is a High School Teacher of Northern City High School, Gulu.

Peko Francis ogaku is a High School Teacher of Literature at Gulu Army Secondary School. He is also coordinator of FEMRITE writing clubs in Gulu.

James Ogoola is the former Principal Judge of the High Court of Uganda and was a Justice of the COMESA Court of Justice in Lusaka, Zambia. His 1st collection of poems; Songs of Paradise: A Harvest of Poetry and Verse, published in 2009 received favourable critical acclaim.

Opio Dokotum Okaka is currently Vice Chancellor, Academic Affairs, at Lira University. He holds a PhD in literature and worked as senior lecturer at Kyambogo University before transfering to Lira. His works of fiction include films, plays, and poetry.

Jennifer A. Okech holds a B.A in Literature, Communication Skills and Linguistics from Makerere University. She is a member of FEMRITE where she has published short stories and poetry.

Okot Benge Holds a PhD in African Literature and currently is Head of Department of Literature at Makerere University. He co-edited the pioneer Uganda Poetry Anthology 2000, a publication of Fountain Publishers.

Jane Okot P'Bitek Langoya is a lawyer by training and holds a MBA (Entrepreneurship and Business Venturing). She is Deputy Registrar General (Registries) at the Uganda Registration Bureau Services. Her first verse publication, *Song of Farewell* (1994), was in the Song tradition pioneered by her father, Okot p'Bitek. Her poetry collection co-authored with Sophie Bamwoyeraki was published in 2016.

Julianne Okot P'Bitek is a poet and scholar. Her essays, short fiction and other poems have been published widely in print and online. Juliane's latest collection of poetry *100 Days* (University of Alberta Press 2016) focuses on the commemoration and memory after genocide. Her PhD research investigates the relationship between memory, history and alienation. Some of her writing can be found at julianeokotbitek.com. She lives with her family in Vancouver, Canada.

Simon Peter Okwir is a High School student and a member of FEMRITE Creative Writing clubs in Gulu.

James Onono Ojok, born in 1988, is a published poet and practicing journalist with Mega Fm Gulu and Acholi Times. In 2008, while at Gulu central High school Onono's poem "Lamunu my mother 'won the second prize in the Femrite Poetry poster project Awards.

Jackson Otim Dre is an artist - actor and writer. He studied Literature at Makerere University. He works with Ideal Solutions, a firm that offers Media Services.

Moses Agaba Rubalema is a high school student and a member of the FEMRITE creative writing club in St Mary's College Rushoroza.
Isaac Settuba is a French Translator and lives in-between two cities; Addis Ababa and Kampala.

Ernest Tashobya Katwesigye is a Christian Lawyer and Writer. He has been a member of the FEMRITE Readers/ Writers' Club since 2003. He has published short stories, poems, theological/Spiritual works and magazine articles. His anthology, Road of Love, co-authored with his wife Zebia, won the 2009/10 National Book Trust Book of the Year – Poetry category.

Isaac Tibasiima is a PhD Student of Literature. He is based at the Department of Literature Makerere University.

James Turyatemba is a published poet. He works with Uganda Examinations Board, Kampala.

Jotham Tusingwire is a published poet. He heads the Department of Literature and English at Ntare School, Mbarara.

Henry 'THB' Twahirwa is an Architect, Painter, and Sculptor who also enjoys writing. He enjoys travelling within and outside Africa. His movements have shaped him into an eclectic person whose work and culture are defined by mixed influences.

Hilda J. Twongyeirwe is a literature professional, an editor and writer. She was chief convener of the inaugural FEMRITE International Literature Conference held at Makerere University, 2016. Hilda works with FEMRITE and is a member of; Action for Development, The Graca Machel Women in Media Network, Association for Women's Rights in Development, and the African Asian Writers Union.

Timothy Wangusa is poet-novelist and a Professor of Literature. He taught at Makerere University and In recent years he has served as Research Professor at Uganda Christian University and as Vice Chancellor of Kumi University. He has produced four volumes of poetry, two novels, and essays. His novel, Upon This Mountain was set literature book on Uganda's syllabus for secondary school.

Subira Yamumpa is a high school student and a member of FEMRITE creative writing Club in Kigezi High School, Kabale.

Printed in the United States
By Bookmasters